SEIZE LIFE NOW
AND
Forever

SEIZE LIFE NOW
AND
Forever

THE BREAKTHROUGH TO UNDERSTANDING 1, 2, AND 3 JOHN

Bible Reading
Breakthrough
VOLUME II

LOU & NICOLE MERTES

Bible Reading Breakthrough™
Bellevue, Washington

Published in 2013 by
Bible Reading Breakthrough™ Press
A division of The Impact Organization, Inc.
500 106th Ave NE, Suite 1801
Bellevue WA 98004
www.Biblereadingbreakthrough.com

All Bible quotations in this publication are taken from the "Revised Standard Version of the Bible," copyright 1952 [2nd edition, 1971] by the Division of Christian Education of the National Council of the Churches of Christ in the United States of America. Used by permission. All rights reserved. All emphasis in Scripture Quotations has been added by the authors.

ISBN 978-0-9832421-1-6 (soft cover)

Library of Congress Control Number: 2013933420

Cover & Interior Design by Scribe Freelance Book Design Company

PUBLISHER CATALOGING IN PUBLICATION INFO

Mertes, Lou & Mertes, Nicole
Seize Life Now and Forever: The Breakthrough to Understanding 1, 2, and 3 John/ Lou Mertes & Nicole Mertes

1.   Bible. N.T.   John—Criticism, interpretation, etc. I Title. II. Volume

2.   Christian life—Biblical teaching   I Title. II. Volume

BS2615   2013

Acknowledgments

We wish to thank the following church scholars and leaders whose writings enabled us to build on their enlightened and foundational insights; for without these fortuitous encounters, this book may never have come to life.

- Peter Ellis for introducing us to structural parallelism
- Fr. John Breck for extending our knowledge of chiastic structures
- John Wesley for affirming our decision to focus on John's letters
- Pope Benedict XVI for affirming the importance of our reading of John's message to seize life now

Peter F. Ellis, Professor Emeritus of New Testament, Fordham University as author of *The Genius of John* effectively demonstrated the existence of structural parallelism in John's writings and its crucial contribution to accurately comprehending scriptural text.

Fr. John Breck, Professor of Patristic Exegesis and Bioethics, St. Sergius Orthodox Theological Institute, Paris, France as author of *The Shape of Biblical Language: Chiasmus in Scriptures and Beyond* noted the spiraling motion found in certain parallel structures that led to our development of the spiral reading method.

John Wesley, the Anglican cleric whose teachings led to the Methodist movement, the Holiness movement, Pentecostalism, and multi-denominational Charismatic movements made numerous journal entries that affirmed our decision to place our attention on John's letters. One of Wesley's journal entries explains his view of the foundational importance of 1 John to Christianity.

> *1 John is the deepest part of Holy Scripture, above all other inspired writings, . . . the plain and full account of genuine Christianity.*

Pope Benedict XVI as author of *Jesus of Nazareth, Part Two,* elegantly summarizes St. John's message when he states eternal life is available within one's own lifetime and emphasizes the importance of living such life (seizing it) now. This inspired us to entitle this book, *Seize Life Now and Forever!*

> *"Eternal life" is not—as the modern reader might immediately assume—life after death, in contrast to this present life, which is transient and not eternal. "Eternal life" is life itself, real life, which can also be lived in the present age and is no longer challenged by physical death. This is the point: to seize "life" here and now, real life that can no longer be destroyed by anything or anyone.*[1]

---

[1] Joseph Ratzinger Pope Benedict XVI, *Jesus of Nazareth, Part Two* (San Francisco: Ignatius Press, 2011) 82.

About the Authors

Lou And Nicole Mertes

Lou and Nicole have served on the Seattle Pacific Seminary Advisory Council and are directors of the Bible Reading Breakthrough™ Project, a ministry dedicated to bringing enthusiasm back to Bible study. Their work enables today's readers:

- To comprehend God's word as the original audiences would have heard and understood it
- To provide more clarity and accuracy of interpretation
- To more fully engage in Bible study and thus receive the transformational effects of God's word

When they are not writing, they, with their grandson, compete in tall building stair climbing fund-raising events.

About Lou

Lou brings the same innovative spirit to Bible study that he was recognized for throughout his career as a chief information executive. He was recognized in *Time Magazine's* 1983 computer of the year issue for spearheading the largest implementation of email and office automation to that date. He authored a *Harvard Business Review* article on that topic, which was one of the most requested reprints. He was invited to speak worldwide and to contribute to the book *Communications in the Twenty-first Century*.

While completing his degree in theology in 2006, Lou saw how to develop an easier and more direct way for today's Bible readers to understand God's word. He has been researching, writing, and teaching about it ever since.

About Nicole

Nicole brings her love of making complex ideas simple and clear to the writing of this book. After she began her career in management, she saw the potential for managers to become innovators and catalysts for change if they could learn how to break through complex processes to implement new and simpler ways to do things. This led to her founding a company to offer instructional and software products for ongoing improvement. During the company's twenty-eight years, thousands of clients received raises, bonuses, and promotions by putting the techniques her company taught into practice.

Nicole was invited to teach at the University of Wisconsin's summer banking program for seven years. This led to the endorsement of her company's vanguard software by the American Bankers Association. Its success as an improvement tool was ultimately featured on the cover of *Quality Digest*.

Nicole is the designer of eight instructional products, one receiving the highest award for instructional excellence from the International Society for Performance and Instruction. Today, she relishes helping people realize the inspiring power of the Bible by breaking through confusing and illogical statements to the elegance and comprehensibility by which it was first heard.

Contents

INTRODUCTION
Seize "Life!"

"Structure . . . is more than an artificial or artistic device . . . It is rather a key to meaning. Not paying sufficient attention to it may result in failure to grasp the true theme."

—Yehuda T. Radday, author of *Chiasmus in Hebrew Biblical Narrative*

CHAPTER 1

What's New!

IS ANYTHING WRONG?

John explains the irrefutable journey to love and eternal life in his three letters. Pastors and scholars alike laud these letters for their superlative passages; however, they also say the letters are confusing in many places. They call them a "difficult read." Yet, when you consider that John's 1st century listeners were for the most part uneducated and illiterate, why do today's readers say the letters are difficult? Implausible as it may seem, John's listening audience *heard* the scriptural text differently than people read the same text today. New biblical research reveals what that difference is.

This book builds on this exciting new research to give you a new reading experience. We will present John's letters the way those early listeners would have heard and understood them. When you read the letters this way, you will discover a 133-verse opus containing the most concise and clear package of Christianity's tenets than anywhere else in the New Testament.

WHAT IS DIFFERENT?

John and other writers of his day used a non-visual framework to reach their listening audience. They did not use any spatial cues such as paragraphs or bullet items to connect or emphasize elements of their writing; their aural audience couldn't have heard such things. Their writing was formatted more like what is in the figure on the next page.

FIGURE 1-1: HOW THE TEXT OF JOHN'S 1ST LETTER MIGHT HAVE APPEARED[2]

To help their audience track what they had to say, 1st century writers did something listeners could hear—they repeated words and phrases. This repetition wasn't necessarily for emphasis or literary ornamentation as people think today; writers such as John used it as a memory aid and as a means to organize what they wrote. For example, John used repetition to:

- Cue the beginning, the end, and the climax of a story.
- Identify important points.
- Connect ideas within a story.

This discovery came by way of research in the literary aspects of the Bible[3] only a few hundred years ago. An important confirming finding arrived early in the twentieth century when the Sumero-Akkadian and Ugaritic literary texts were discovered. These ancient tablets indicated the Semitic people of John's time had been steeped in writing this way for

---

[3] Nils Wilhelm Lund, *Chiasmus In The New Testament: A Study in the Form and Function of Chiastic Structures* (Hendrickson Publishers, Inc. reprinted by arrangement with the University of North Carolina Press, 1992) 33.

thousands of years.[4] Children actually learned the alphabet forwards and backwards and from the extremities toward the middle in order to deal with the form of writing that was used then.[5]

We will look at the rhetorical form biblical scholars refer to as *chiasm*. While it may sound rather esoteric, it isn't. It directly impacts what you will get out of reading John's epistles!

THIS ISN'T THE WAY WE LEARNED TO READ

Verse numbers that make the Bible's writing look linear were inserted by an interpreter in the sixteenth century.[6] Modern readers follow these verse numbers reading from top to bottom expecting this straight-line structure to make sense, but in many cases, it does not. As you will soon see, the fundamental organization of John's letters is not in a straight line.

Twenty-first century people are overwhelmingly visual learners and sequential thinkers who do *not* naturally pair bits of data that are out of linear sequence. To put this bluntly, we read in a straight line what biblical authors intended for us to assimilate in a completely different way!

AN EXAMPLE

A passage from Matthew provides an excellent example of the type of structure John used throughout his writing. It illustrates the difference between what today's readers take in using their 21st century reading style and what 1st century listeners would have naturally apprehended. Read what Jesus said below. What did he say the swine do?

FIGURE 1-1: MATTHEW 7:6

"Do not give dogs what is holy; and do not throw your pearls before swine, lest they trample them under foot and turn to attack you" (Mt 7:6).

---

[4] Isaac Mendelsohn, editor, *Religions of the Ancient Near East: Sumero-Akkadian Religious Texts and Ugaritic Epics.* (Liberal Arts Press, 1955).

[5] John Breck, *The Shape of Biblical language: Chiasmus in the Scriptures and Beyond* (St. Vladimir's Seminary Press, 1994) 29.

[6] http://www.bible-researcher.com/chapter-verse.html.

Most people answer the swine trample the pearls and turn to attack you, but if this were the case, why introduce the topic of the dogs? First-century listeners would have said the dogs were the attackers *not* the swine. What explains the difference?

Even though they would have heard the verse as it is depicted in Figure 1–1, they would have comprehended the verse as a spiral, *not* a straight line. They would have paired the first part of the verse with the last part to say the dogs, not the swine, would attack. Scholars call this type of first-last organization a *chiastic structure,*[7] whereby **A** is paired with **A'** and **B** is paired with **B'** to be read in an **A: A': B: B'** sequence.

FIGURE 1–2: MATTHEW 7:6 IN STRUCTURAL FORM

A Do not give dogs what is holy
   B and do not throw your pearls before swine,
   B' lest they trample them under foot
A' and turn to attack you (Mt 7:6).

Scholar John Breck calls this type of reading sequence *spiral reading* because it moves spiral like from the first point to the last and finishes in the center. He explained why spiral reading is of such importance.

The real meaning of the passage cannot be discerned unless we read it "spirally," from the extremities toward the center . . .[8]

The figure below depicts the spiral text that was derived from the **A: A': B: B'** reading sequence. Read it to see how much easier it is to understand than the rendition we depicted in Figure 1–1.

---

[7] M. Eugene Boring, Contributor, *The New Interpreter's Bible Volume VIII* (Abingdon Press, 1995) 212

[8] John Breck, *The Shape of Biblical language: Chiasmus in the Scriptures and Beyond* (St. Vladimir's Seminary Press, 1994) 29.

FIGURE 1–3: MATTHEW 7:6 IN SPIRAL FORM

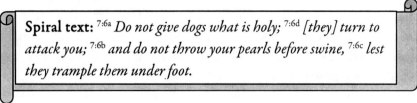

Spiral text: [7:6a] *Do not give dogs what is holy;* [7:6d] *[they] turn to attack you;* [7:6b] *and do not throw your pearls before swine,* [7:6c] *lest they trample them under foot.*

Jesus could have said this differently, but Matthew does not cite him as doing so. Why did Jesus speak this way? We can only conclude that this was what people of the 1st century were used to.

OUR PURPOSE

Our purpose is to bring John's "invisible" structures to light by sequencing the passages the same way John's original audience would have mentally assembled the information. You will not need to be concerned with structural notations like **A**'s and **B**'s. You will simply read the spiral text as you normally read scriptural text. We will provide comments to help you assimilate John's writing with the same congruity, consistency, and clarity his 1st century audience would have enjoyed.

THE ADVANTAGE OF THE HOLISTIC VIEW

Missing any part of John's letters because the text is confusing leads to a huge loss. It would be like experiencing only the four-note motif (short, short, short, long—da-da-da-dum) of Beethoven's Fifth without ever

hearing its many variations that are contained in the entire symphony.[9]
John's three letters are like a symphony. Composers arrange three-note chords in variation after variation to move their listening audience. John's goal was to move his listening audience too, and he did through variations of his three-part word-chords.

---

[9]http://en.wikipedia.org/w/index.php?title=File:Beethoven_symphony_5_opening.svg&page=1

Like Beethoven, John's genius lies in how he arranged his word-chords. In his first letter, he wove the idea of eternal life into sixty-nine intricately connected variations to explain God's plan for its restoration. John wrote so that people could to take his words right off the page and place them into their minds and hearts to live what God says to do!

A SHORT OVERVIEW

John organizes his letters the way today's journalists would, with the who, what, why, when, where, and how of God's plan. Nowhere else in the Bible will you find such a tight yet cohesive presentation of Christianity's New Covenant and its blueprint for implementation.

- **What** is the purpose of God's plan—eternal life.
- **Who** has the opportunity to receive it—everyone who believes in Jesus' name.
- **When** is it available—now, in one's own lifetime.
- **Where** will it happen—right here on earth.
- **How** God implements it—through the incarnation, death, and resurrection of his Son, Jesus Christ.
- **How** to receive it—believe in Jesus' name and love one another.
- **Why** did God initiate the plan—because God is love and loves the world.

THE PARADIGM SHIFT

Christianity brought a radical idea. Until Jesus proved otherwise, everyone died at the end of their physical life. End of story. However, Jesus' defeat of death demonstrated the eternality of life that led to a paradigm shift that still rocks the world.

When God sent Jesus, he upped his offer via a new covenant, not for the Israelites alone but for all humanity. He restored eternal life without asking humans to do anything more than he had always asked of them. From the beginning, his command was to love one another, and humans have always had freewill choice about keeping his command. God sent Jesus to give them aid and demonstrate a more powerful reason to live a loving life in their one and only lifetime.

THE KINDS OF THINGS YOU WILL LEARN

Read these letters for a clear answer to what the New Covenant is and requires of humankind. John's answer is crisp, yet without sacrifice of the details. He could have stopped when he said it is necessary to love one another but he doesn't. He goes on to explain how to fulfill this command successfully.

Many Christians blithely state they believe in Jesus' name, but we wonder how many actually realize there are three parts to Jesus' name—Jesus the man, the Son of God, and the Christ. John explains their distinct functions and why all three are needed.

He also explains why becoming a child of God through Jesus will be different from the way the people of Israel received this gift. It is vital for Christians to understand this because the new plan calls for their active participation. The Israelites inherited their child of God status as a birthright, but now, individuals by their freewill choices determine their destiny.

THE BIG NEWS OF THESE LETTERS

John repeatedly emphasizes God's plan is for people to have access to eternal life in their lifetime! He encourages his audience of believers to love one another, which is what it takes to live their life with God now.

> *Beloved let us love one another; for love is of God, and he who loves is born of God and knows God. He who does not love does not know God; for God is love* (1Jn 4:7–8).

John would not have said, "He who loves is born of God and knows God" in the present tense, if he did *not* mean you could receive assurance of eternal life in the ever present now. Why do we say seize life now? It is because the only life you have to live on a love-filled basis is your current life. If a person does not follow this path, life ends in permanent death as if Jesus had never walked the earth. Pope Benedict XVI states it this way:

> *"Eternal life" is not—as the modern reader might immediately assume—life after death, in contrast to this present life, which is transient and not eternal. "Eternal life" is*

life itself, real life, which can also be lived in the present age and is no longer challenged by physical death. This is the point: to seize "life" here and now, real life that can no longer be destroyed by anything or anyone.[10]

THE ISSUE OF FAITH

Ultimately, John said receiving eternal life is about having faith.

Who is it that overcomes the world but he who believes that Jesus is the Son of God and this is the victory that overcomes the world, our faith (1Jn 5:5; 4b).

We encourage you to take John's letters to heart because John is an eyewitness to Jesus. He is one of the most qualified to testify to who Jesus is—John was with him from the beginning to the end.

Faith for Christians starts from the testimony of another—a parent, pastor, or friend, to name the more common sources. They are all human! The only way to have faith in Jesus is to first trust what another person says. Even the authors of Scriptures were human. Consider how potent the words would be coming from someone like John who had been with Jesus under the following circumstances.

- He was with Jesus from the beginning.

    "And you also are witnesses, because you have been with me from the beginning" (Jn 15:27).

- He was at the foot of the cross, where Jesus entrusted his mother to him.

    When Jesus saw his mother, and the disciple whom he loved standing near, he said . . . to the disciple, "Behold your mother!" (Jn 19:26).

---

[10] Joseph Ratzinger Pope Benedict XVI, *Jesus of Nazareth, Part Two* (San Francisco: Ignatius Press, 2011) 82.

- He was with Jesus after he resurrected.

  On the evening of that day, the first day of the week . . . where the disciples were . . . Jesus came and stood among them (Jn 20:19).

- He received the Holy Spirit directly from Jesus.

  He breathed on them and said to them, "Receive the Holy Spirit" (Jn 20:22).

- He was commanded by Jesus to testify.

  "As the Father has sent me, even so I send you" (Jn 20:21b).

- John presents his testimony in his letters

  . . . And we saw it, and testify to it, and proclaim to you the eternal life, which was with the Father (1Jn 1:2b).

Given his experiences, you can see how the fire of John's passion built the faith of his listeners, and we hope it will for you too.

WHY READ JOHN'S LETTERS?

John explains the crucial foundational information about Christianity (reason #1) in an accessible format so everyone can "get it" (reason #2). John was an eyewitness; he was there to see, hear, and experience Jesus as the human, the Son of God, and the Christ (reason#3). The compelling power behind John's words is sure to find its way into a receptive reader's heart and mind (reason #4).

HOW THIS BOOK HELPS YOU

We write to enable you to understand John's letters with your 21st-century eyes, mind, and heart. We will help you cross the 2,000-year cultural divide of language and worldview. We will:

- Arrange the scriptural text in *spiral form* as 1st-century listeners would have comprehended it.
- Provide information about the meaning of Greek words when simple translations to English are not enough.
- Provide information about words that John uses to convey a special theological meaning.
- Insert passages from John's Gospel and the Old Testament to shed more light on the message of the letter.
- Provide tables to compare and contrast key points.
- Provide background about parallel structuralism and chiasm in the appendices where we will also display the structures of John's three epistles. This is for those who want to see how the spiral text was assembled; it is *not* required to understand this book.

Our purpose is to make your reading experience as fruitful and efficient as possible. John's embedded structures are the missing link to understanding his letters. They have been lost for probably 1,700 years and now, gratefully, are found. Richard Moulton, a 19th-century literary scholar at the University of Chicago, brought the existence of structured parallelism and chiastic structures in the Bible to the forefront. He believed when the structures are visible the reader will not need another's interpretation.

> *The essential thing is that the verse structure should be represented to the eye . . . where structural arrangement is wanting, no amount of explanation is likely to be of much avail.*[11]

The spiral text we display in this book answers Moulton's requirement. Next, we will address a second preparatory topic—John's overall organization and the ultimate meaning of his letters.

---

[11] Richard G. Moulton, *The Literary Study of the Bible* (London: Heath & Co., 1898) 45.

"The life was made manifest, and we saw it, and testify to it, and proclaim to you the eternal life, which was with the Father and was made manifest to us" (1 Jn 1:2).

CHAPTER 2

The Organization of the Letters

JOHN'S ULTIMATE MEANING

Typically, modern readers wait to discover the ultimate meaning of a work through their reading of it, but Johannine scholar C. H. Dodd advises the opposite. He says readers of John would benefit from advance knowledge of his major theme.

> *Accurate interpretation of the whole depends upon precise understanding of the text in light of the ultimate meaning of the work.*[12]

While Dodd's comments are directed to readers of John's Gospel, his maxim also holds for John's letters. However, when you read the first letter linearly, John's key idea is *not* easy to discern. He covers so many topics one after another, you wonder where he is headed. Some say the key idea is love, others say it is fellowship; others say it is to warn about the antichrists, but John himself tells you what it is.

JOHN'S BRILLIANT USE OF THE GREEK WORD *ANGELIA* FOR MESSAGE

John does it through his use of the Greek word *angelia*. This word is used only twice in the entire New Testament, both by John in the first letter. According to scholar Raymond Brown, *angelia* refers to a special type of message: it is a message that conveys good news.[13] Indeed, John has good news to convey! His news is God's restoration of humanity's opportunity to receive assurance of eternal life in the here and now of their lifetime. This is the ultimate meaning that is the foundation of all three of John's letters.

---

[12] C. H. Dodd, *The Interpretation of the Fourth Gospel* (Cambridge University Press, 1953) 3.

[13] Raymond E. Brown, Translation with Introduction, Notes, and Commentary, *The Anchor Bible: The Epistles of John* (New York: Doubleday, 1982) 193.

John uses *angelia* to point to the New Covenant that God makes through his Son Jesus. The two parts of the covenant are the connecting threads that unify all the elements of John's letters. Only two passages begin with, *This is the message* (*angelia*). They convey the following two parts of the covenant.

| What God provides | ⟸⟹ | What people do to receive it |

A linear reading of the letter will *not* reveal what John so brilliantly did with *angelia*. It takes a spiral reading to see the structural parallelism that *angelia* cues. Its first use points to God's side of the equation—what he provides; its second use points to the believer's side of the equation—what he or she must do. John organizes his entire first letter around these two parts.

TABLE 2-1. THE "GOOD NEWS" MESSAGE IS THE NEW COVENANT

THE TWO PARTIES OF THE AGREEMENT	"THIS IS THE MESSAGE" PASSAGES	EXPLANATION
What God provides	*This is the message* (*angelia*) *we have heard from him and proclaim to you, that God is light and in him is no darkness at all, and the blood of Jesus his Son cleanses us from all sin. We . . . proclaim to you the eternal life.* (1 Jn 1:5; 7b; 2b)	This is the announcement of the restoration of eternal life! In addition, John says God sent his Son to cleanse the sins of those who wish to have eternal life.
What humankind does	*For* ***this is the message*** (*angelia*), *which you have heard from the beginning that we should love one another* (1 Jn 3:11).	Through their love of God, believers receive eternal life by keeping God's command to love by living a love-based life.

John uses the first message as one rail of a track to convey who God is, what he does, and when; he uses the second message as a second rail to convey what humanity does. Everything John writes in the first letter falls onto one rail or the other. John's ultimate message of eternal life is like a train that rolls on two rails to the final destination of having fellowship with God.

WHAT THIS MEANS FOR YOU

Without an awareness of the letter's two rails and the methodical way John answers the who, what, why, where, and how of the good news of eternal life, the first letter will appear to be a scramble of facts and advice that, while useful, does not seem to cohere around anything, but through the repetition of *angelia*, John tells you exactly what he is up to.

John's mission is for people to do what they need to do to receive the assurance of eternal life in their own lifetime.

> *I write to you who believe in the name of the Son of God, that*
> *you may know that you have eternal life* (1Jn 5:13).

This passage implies two things: you know how to receive eternal life and you are confident that you are living it after God grants it. You can look forward to more information on these topics when you get into the first letter.

THE PRIMARY CONCEPTS BEHIND GOD'S PLAN

John uses several important concepts to describe God's plan. A concept is a notion or idea that we formulate in our 21st-century minds based on our 21st-century exposures and life experiences. For example, our notions of truth, faith, love, and sin are, for the most part, personal constructions based on today's world. However, the reader of John needs to know where John was coming from.

The reader who understands these key concepts as John uses them in his letters, will touch the roots of Christianity's theology. Whether or not what John says lines up exactly with your current beliefs or those of the religious system you follow, these roots will help you assess the theological implications of the rest of the New Testament. The word *theology* means religious or divine truth so we will start with the concept of truth.

WHAT IS THE TRUTH?

When Jesus told Pilate that he came to bear witness to the truth, what did he mean? When he said everyone one who is of the truth hears his voice, what did he mean? Pilate wanted to know about truth just as we do when he asked, "What is the truth?"

> *"For this I was born, and for this I have come into the world, to bear witness to the truth. Everyone who is of the truth hears my voice." Pilate said to him, "What is the truth?"* (Jn 18:37c– 38a).

When Jesus says he came to the world to bear witness to the truth, he is saying he came to bear witness to God in two specific ways.

1. Jesus bears witness to the fact God sent him to bring eternal life to the world.

   > *"And I know that his commandment is eternal life. What I say, therefore, I say as the father has bidden me"* (Jn 12:50).

2. Jesus bears witness to the truth when he issues the command to love one another. Since Jesus only says what the Father has bidden him, this command is Jesus' witness to the Father's desire for humankind to love one another.

   > *"A new commandment I give to you, that you love one another"* (Jn 13:34a).

These two statements of the truth are the essence of the New Covenant. They represent the message that is the good news that John announces by his use of the word *angelia*. In condensed form it is as follows:

^{4:12}*God gave us eternal life...*

If we

...^{3:23}*believe in the name of his Son Jesus Christ and love one another...*

WHY FAITH IN JESUS IS SO IMPORTANT

An attack on Jesus' identity as the incarnate Son of God is a big deal. Such an attack casts doubt on the very reason God sent his Son to the world.

> *"The Father who sent me has himself given me commandment what to say and what to speak. And I know that his commandment is eternal life"* (Jn 12: 49b–50).

If a person doubts that Jesus makes eternal life possible, why should he or she believe what he said or did? Disbelief puts into question the ultimate power of love and the very existence of life after death for which Jesus incarnated, died, and resurrected. John, as an eyewitness of Jesus' defeat of death and a recipient of eternal life, writes to dispel any doubt about Jesus.

JESUS BEARS WITNESS TO LOVE

The truth as Jesus states it, is the imperative to love in order to receive eternal life. God loves the world and Jesus tells those of the world to love one another.

> *For God so loved the world that he gave his only Son . . . that the world might be saved through him* (Jn 3:16–17).

Those who believe in Jesus as God's Son would *not* ignore his commandment, especially knowing the source is from God. Therefore, you could say that to believe in Jesus' name is to make a commitment to love. It is the crucial requirement for eternal life.

Jesus is the linchpin of God's plan for eternal life. God sent him to bear witness to this truth. The route to eternal life is through love because God is love and Jesus represents God.

I am the way, the truth, and the life; no one comes to the Father,
but by me (Jn 14:6).

WHAT IS SIN?

John defines sin as all wrongdoing; however, he differentiates between sin
that leads to death—mortal sin—and sin that does not lead to death—non-
mortal sin.

> *All wrongdoing is sin, but there is sin, which is not mortal* (1Jn
> 5:17).

Those who have received assurance of eternal life do not commit mortal sin
because having eternal life is to live forever. Therefore, once a person
receives assurance of eternal life, he or she does not commit mortal sins that
would lead to death.

What would such sins be? Although John does not provide a detailed
list of such sins, we do know mortal sin is a breach or transgression of divine
law. John is quite clear about what the divine law is under God's new plan.
It comes in the form of a new commandment.

THE NEW COMMANDMENT

The new commandment has two parts. John calls the requirement to love
one another the old part because his listeners have heard it from the
beginning. God's sending his Son Jesus Christ is reason for the new part,
which is as follows.

> *. . . we should believe in the name of his Son Jesus Christ . . .*
> (1Jn 3:23).

In the prologue of his Gospel, John said that those who believe in
Jesus' name receive the right to receive eternal life. Many people miss the
fact, that John is *not* saying they will receive eternal life by belief in Jesus'
name; he is only saying they receive the *right* to receive it.

> *But . . . to those who believe in his name: to them he gave the*
> *right to become children of God* (Jn 1:12).

The new commandment answers how to convert the right into an actuality. It is to love one another as God commanded from the beginning! The basis for receiving eternal life is therefore, for believers to develop a lifestyle of thoughts, words, and deeds that come from loving intentions.

NOW IT IS TIME TO READ 1 JOHN

We have introduced you to the abridged version of God's plan. We have sketched what eternal life is and provided a brief look at how to receive it. Now, for the first time ever, you have the opportunity to read John's complete message as his community heard and comprehended it!

The Gift of Eternal Life

CHAPTER 3

The Word of Life
Spiral Text (1:1–7; 5:18–21)

INTRODUCTION

This is the first part of a three-part letter. In it, John previews the New Covenant and God's plan to implement it. In just eleven verses, John will cover the elemental principles of Christianity!

He opens straight-on with his purpose, which concerns the *word of life*, whom John personally saw, heard, and touched. During that occasion, the resurrected Jesus breathed eternal life on John and the disciples giving them the Holy Spirit. This gift of eternal life is what John writes about; it represents a life-giving turning point for the world!

John covers what Jesus came to do, why it was necessary, and the eternal life humanity has the opportunity to receive. John's discourse when read in spiral text form, is persuasive, logical, and strikingly clear just as John's 1st century audience would have heard it.

John paints a sensate world of choice points—of dark or light, death or life, sin or love, lies or truth that lead to *the* fundamental question of the letter—will you choose to walk in the light or not? As an eyewitness, John proclaims eternal fellowship with God has been restored through Jesus, and he personally attests to its joy and amazing benefits.

To track with what John says, look for the following terms he uses for eternal life:

- Fellowship with the Father and his Son Jesus Christ
- To be born of God
- To be in him who is true

John concludes with a summary piece of advice. He says, "Keep yourselves from idols." Indeed, he makes as compelling case for doing so! Now, we invite you to read John's Spirit guided words for yourself.

SPIRAL TEXT

ORIENTATION

Read the spiral text below to get started with this chapter. We will display each portion of this text with scriptural reference points, Greek word meaning, and explanatory notations as we proceed through this chapter.

1 JOHN 1:1–7; 5:18–21

Fellowship with God

[1:1a]That, which was from the beginning, [1c]concerning the word of life, [1b]which we have heard, which we have seen with our eyes, which we have looked upon and touched with our hands. [1:3]That which we have seen and heard we proclaim also to you so that you may have fellowship with us and our fellowship is with the Father and with his Son Jesus Christ.

Walk in the Light

[1:5]This is the message we have heard from him and proclaim to you, that God is light and in him is no darkness at all [7b]and the blood of Jesus his Son cleanses us from all sin.

[1:6]If we say we have fellowship with him while we walk in darkness, we lie and do not live according to the truth; [7a]but if we walk in the light as he is in the light, we have fellowship with him. [4]And we are writing this that your joy may be complete.

The Gift of Eternal Life

[1:2a]The life was made manifest, [2c]which was with the Father and was made manifest to us. [2b]We saw it and testify to it, and proclaim to you the eternal life.

The Benefits of Eternal Life

[5:18a]We know that any one born of God does not sin. [19]We know that we are of God, and the whole world is in the power of the evil one, [18b]but he who was born of God keeps him, and the evil one does not touch him. [20]And we know that the Son of God has come and has given us understanding, to know him who is true; and we are in him who is true, in his Son Jesus Christ. This is the true God and eternal life.

The Challenge

[5:21]Little children, keep yourselves from idols.

COMMENTARY

FELLOWSHIP WITH GOD

Spiral text: [1:1a]That which was from the beginning, [1c]concerning the word of life, [1b]which we have heard, which we have seen with our eyes, which we have looked upon and touched with our hands. [1:3]That which we have seen and heard we proclaim also to you so that you may have fellowship with us and our fellowship is with the Father and with his Son Jesus Christ.

JOHN WRITES OF THE WORD OF LIFE

John opens this letter powerfully through his reference to that which was from the beginning. He directs our attention to the Word of life, who was with God from the beginning and who John and the disciples have heard, seen, and touched with their own hands!

> *In the beginning was the Word, and the Word was with God,*
> *and the Word was God* (Jn 1:1).

John is referring to the third day, when the resurrected Jesus came to the disciples and they knew without a doubt he was the Word of life. This is when the glorified Jesus gave them eternal life.

Jesus came and stood among them and said to them, "Peace be with you."... he showed them his hands and his side ... Jesus said to them again ... "As the Father has sent me, even so I send you." And when he had said this, he breathed on them, and said to them, "Receive the Holy Spirit." (Jn 20: 19–22).

As one of the very few to receive this initial restoration of eternal life, John clearly has authority to proclaim the message of eternal life. Indeed, Jesus commanded the disciples to do so.

WHY DOES JOHN MENTION FELLOWSHIP?

When John says he and the disciples have *fellowship* with the Father and his Son Jesus, he is speaking of much more than a social relationship. He refers to having the ongoing communion with God that is eternal life.

And this is eternal life, that they know thee the only true God, and Jesus Christ whom thou has sent (Jn 17:3).

John writes this letter to proclaim eternal life so that all believers may join the disciples' perpetual *fellowship* with the Father and his Son.

God's plan for this actually hinges on the disciples' testimony, for only by their testimony can people know of its availability. In this letter, John will do more than announce eternal life; he will address how one receives it, which he broaches next.

WALK IN THE LIGHT

Spiral text: [1:5]This is the message we have heard from him and proclaim to you, that God is light and in him is no darkness at all [7b]and the blood of Jesus his Son cleanses us from all sin.

[1:6]If we say we have fellowship with him while we walk in darkness, we lie and do not live according to the truth; [7a]but if we walk in the light as he is in the light, we have fellowship with him. [4]And we are writing this that your joy may be complete.

THE ISSUE OF DARKNESS (SIN)

John proclaims God is 100% light. There is not one iota of darkness in him. John's point is that sin (darkness) is the problem. For people to live in eternal fellowship with God who is 100% light, John is saying they must deal with their sin. The question is how.

THE SOLUTION

Jesus is the solution. His defeat of death made it possible for people to believe he is the Son of God—the Word of life. When they do, Jesus forgives all of the sins they committed up to that point. He gives them a fresh start without the burden of past sins.

> *You know that he appeared to take away sins, and in him there is no sin* (1 Jn 3:5).

> *"I have come as light into the world, that whoever believes in me may not remain in darkness"* (Jn 12:46).

The question is how to go forward? How does one live after coming to belief in Jesus?

WALK IN THE LIGHT

John's answer is to walk in the light as Jesus is in the light.

> *But he who does what is true comes to the light . . .* (Jn 3:21a).

John correlates walking in the light to living according to the truth, which refers to keeping God's commandments.

> *I rejoiced greatly to find some of your children following the truth, just as we have been commanded by the Father* (2Jn 1:4).

The Father commanded only two things—to believe in the name of his Son and love one another. Since John writes to those who are already believers, he is saying the only other crucial step is to love one another.

And this is his commandment, that we should believe in the name of his Son Jesus Christ and love one another, just as he has commanded us (1Jn 3:23).

If the key to eternal life is to love one another, does this mean people must be perfect to have fellowship with God? The answer is no. John will cover this in the verses to come. John's primary emphasis at this early stage of the letter is to announce eternal life and what it will bring.

YOUR JOY WILL BE COMPLETE

Walking in the light will bring joy, *chara*,[14] which is the complete and abounding gladness that only being with one's creator can bring. Up to this point, the world has not known this kind of ceaseless joy. Before Jesus arrived, there was no fellowship with God; life ended in permanent death— end of story. But now, the Word of life, Jesus has restored the opportunity for humanity to receive the greatest gift of all—joyous life with God.

Before we leave this passage, note the tense of the verb that John uses for the completion of this joy. It is the present tense, which indicates that eternal life is available in the here and now of one's lifetime. We will come back to this phenomenal idea at the end of this chapter.

THE GIFT OF ETERNAL LIFE

Spiral text: [1:2a]The life was made manifest, [2c]which was with the Father and was made manifest to us. [2b]We saw it and testify to it, and proclaim to you the eternal life.

THE DISCIPLES RECEIVED THE "LIFE"

John returns to the awesome fact that after dying on the cross, Jesus was visibly alive on that third day encounter with the disciples. This is what John attests to. In addition to seeing the resurrected Jesus, the disciples experienced the glorified Jesus' breath of eternal life.

However, even with John's sacred testimony, some might question whether the disciples actually received eternal life. Close reading only

---

[14] http://classic.net.bible.org/strong.php?id=4137.

indicates that Jesus gave the disciples the Holy Spirit. How do we know eternal life came with that breath?

Prophets have received the Spirit through the ages, but they did not live eternally. Leviticus Rabbah an ancient commentary on Hebrew scripture[15] confirms this when it states that the prophets only received the Holy Spirit by measure.

> *The Holy Spirit rested on the prophets by measure* (Leviticus Rabbah 15:2).

Contrast this to John the Baptist's statement that Jesus gives the Spirit without measure.

> *". . . for it is not without measure that he gives the Spirit;"* (Jn 3:34b).

In the New Testament also, special people received the Spirit for special circumstances, but they did not receive eternal life. Examples from Luke are: Zechariah (Lk 1:67), Elizabeth (Lk 1:41), and Simeon (Lk 2:25). Other authors associate the Holy Spirit with the granting of special assistance and gifts, but in John's vernacular, the granting of the Holy Spirit always refers the granting of eternal life by Jesus. The evidence of the linkage between Jesus and his granting eternal life through the Holy Spirit is compelling.

EVIDENCE THAT JESUS GAVE THE DISCIPLES ETERNAL LIFE THROUGH THE HOLY SPIRIT

1. John the Baptist tells us God sent Jesus to baptize with the Holy Spirit and that Jesus holds nothing back when he gives the Spirit, meaning he gives eternal life.

    > *". . . for it is not without measure that he gives the Spirit;"* (Jn 3:34b).

---

[15] http://classic.net.bible.org/verse.php?book=Joh&chapter=3&verse=34

2. Jesus confirms that living water (eternal life) will be available to those who believe.

> *"He who believes in me, as the scripture has said, 'Out of his heart shall flow rivers of living water.'" Now this he said about the Spirit, which those who believed in him were to receive; for as yet the Spirit has not been given, because Jesus was not yet glorified* (Jn 7:38–39).

3. In Jesus' Farewell Prayer, he states that God has given him the power to give eternal life and he announces that the hour has arrived to do so. Matthew also records Jesus as stating he will give to those he chooses the ability to *know* God.

> *. . . he lifted his eyes to heaven and said, "Father, the hour has come; . . . since thou hast given him power over all flesh, to give eternal life to all whom thou hast given him"* (Jn 17:1).

> *. . . "And no one knows the Father except the Son and any one to whom the Son chooses to reveal him"* (Mt 11:27c).

4. The most awesome point of confirmation arrives through the particular Greek word John uses for *breathed on* when Jesus gave the Spirit to the disciples.

> *. . . and when he had said this, he <u>breathed on</u> (emphusao) them, and said to them, "Receive the Holy Spirit"* (Jn 20:21–22).

The word *emphusao*[16] occurs only here in the entire New Testament. Its significance lies in its use in the Septuagint (the Greek version of the Old Testament) for God breathing everlasting life into Adam.

---

[16] http://classic.net.bible.org/strong.php?id=1720.

> *. . . then the Lord God formed man of dust from the ground,*
> *and <u>breathed</u> (emphusao) into his nostrils the breath of life;*
> *. . .* (Gen 2:7).

The juxtaposition of *emphusao* at these two life-giving moments[17] establishes that Jesus' gift of the Holy Spirit also includes the gift of eternal life because in both instances eternal life is given. However, in the case of Adam and Eve, God rescinded the eternality of their life when he banished them from the Garden of Eden.

> *". . . the man has now become like one of us, knowing good and*
> *evil; and now, lest he put forth his hand and take also the tree of*
> *life, and eat, and live forever"—therefore the Lord God sent*
> *him forth from the garden of Eden. . .* (Gen 3:22–23).

This banishment led to the onset of the period when eternal life was not available. However, God has given Jesus the authority to restore eternal life, and his glorification marked its commencement.

SUMMARY

Only Jesus the glorified Word of life has the authority to grant eternal life and according to John, this he does through the Holy Spirit. However, outside of John's letters and gospel, you will read about others who baptize with the Holy Spirit. You will find people being filled with the Spirit who manifest special gifts and witness to Jesus. These mentions of the Holy Spirit are in many forms that are reflected in the variety of protocols and sacraments of different Christian denominations. Their bishops, ministers, and others carry the power forward to grant the Holy Spirit as a source of aid to believers on their journey to God.

However, only Jesus grants the eternal life, by which a person becomes born of God.

---

[17] John R. Levison, *Filled With The Spirit*, (Grand Rapids, MI: Wm. B. Eerdmans Publishing Co., 2009) 368–370.

John's reference to the Holy Spirit in his writings is in association with Jesus' granting this ultimate gift.

COMPLETE JOY IS THE OUTCOME

The decision to follow Jesus' call to the light is ultimately up to each individual. We have already discussed the complete joy and abounding gladness that accompanies the receipt of eternal life. As someone who has received eternal life, John proceeds to tell us what causes this complete joy.

THE BENEFITS OF ETERNAL LIFE

Spiral text: [5:18a]We know that any one born of God does not sin. [19]We know that we are of God, and the whole world is in the power of the evil one, [18bc]but he who was born of God keeps him and the evil one does not touch him. [20]And we know that the Son of God has come and has given us understanding, to know him who is true; and we are in him who is true, in his Son Jesus Christ. This is the true God and eternal life.

WHAT THE DISCIPLES *KNOW*

John, having received eternal life, speaks emphatically about what he now *knows*. The Holy Spirit brings deeper insight into divine things; it expands one's ability to *know*.

> "When the, the Spirit of truth, comes, he will guide you into all truth;... (Jn 16:13).

John *knows* Jesus is the Son of God; he is the true God. He is eternal life and John *knows* those who are born of God, which is granted at Jesus' discretion, receive the following benefits.

- They have eternal life.
- They will no longer commit mortal sin.
- They are under God's protection while they are in the world where the evil one reigns; the evil one cannot touch them.
- They will not lose eternal life; they keep God forever.

With these magnificent benefits, it is no wonder that the joy that comes of being born of God is so great. Let us look more closely at each of the last three items.

THOSE BORN OF GOD DO NOT SIN

It will be difficult to find anyone who completely stops committing all sinful behavior after being born of God. Even the stories of the saints attest to this; so what is John saying here? To understand, we need to look ahead to another part of this letter where John differentiates between two types of sin. Only one type is pertinent to John's declaration.

> *There is sin which is mortal; . . . All wrongdoing is sin, but there is sin, which is not mortal* (1 Jn 5:16–17).

Mortal sins are the sins that preclude access to eternal life; they are sins that are so harmful they lead to the perpetrator's permanent death, which is the permanent separation from God.

> *". . . and now, lest he put forth his hand and take also of the tree of life, and eat, and live forever . . ."* (Gen 3:22).

> *He who does not love abides in death* (1 Jn 3:14b).

Those who are born of God do not commit these sins; otherwise, they would not have eternal life—they would die. However, this does lead to the question, how do they manage not to commit these sins?

THEY HAVE GOD'S GREATNESS IN THEM

John states the world is entirely subject to the rule of evil with the striking exception of those who are born of God. They are able to abstain from mortal sin because God protects them. Jesus prayed to the Father for such protection from the evil one in his Farewell Address.

> *"I do not pray that thou shouldst take them out of the world, but that thou should keep them from the evil one . . . I have sent them out into the world. . . . I do not pray for these only, but also*

for those who believe in me through their word . . ." (Jn 17:15;
18; 20).

John affirms this is the case for those who are born of God.

". . . for he who is in you is greater than he who is in the world"
(1 Jn 4:4).

ETERNAL LIFE IS PERMANENT

With mortal sin off the table, John is saying those born of God are not at
risk of losing their eternal life with God. However, how can this be true
when freewill is operable now as it originally was with Adam and Eve? Evil
deceived Adam and Eve, and they chose to act against God; couldn't this
happen now?

The issue is not freewill, rather it is the choices one makes with it. Adam
and Eve chose not to love God enough to respect the one thing he asked
them to do. This time, however, eternal life becomes available in a different
sequence—when believers demonstrate their commitment to love by the
choices they make before they receive the gift of spiritual rebirth, they receive
permanent eternal life. Adam and Eve did *not* choose to receive this gift
before God gave it to them; they chose against it after they had it.

TABLE 3-1. COMPARISON OF ETERNAL LIFE AVAILABILITY BEFORE AND AFTER JESUS

PHASE	ORIGINAL GRANTING OF ETERNAL LIFE TO ADAM AND EVE	WHEN JESUS GRANTS ETERNAL LIFE TO PEOPLE NOW
One	Adam and Eve received everlasting life without asking	Humans first step up to choose to believe in Jesus' name and keep his love commandment
Two	To keep eternal life, Adam and Eve were required to obey God's commandment	Then they receive everlasting life and never lose it

With God's new plan, everyone has the opportunity to exercise his or her freewill to choose God. When love is the clear choice, God answers with a fellowship he will not revoke, which can occur while one is living, just as it did for the disciples. When John states those who are born of God keep God, the verb *keeps* is in the present tense.

> *But he who was born of God keeps him* (1 Jn 5:18b).

THE CHALLENGE

Spiral text: [21]Little children, keep yourselves from idols.

IDOLATRY IS THE CHALLENGE

Believers who are not yet born of God continue to battle the temptations of the world. They are vulnerable to succumbing to the power of people and things that would steal their loyalty away from God. John directly tells them to protect themselves from these "idols."

An idol is anything in the world that people treat as God; they may worship, depend upon, and substitute it for God. Idolatry is broader than most people realize. When people choose something that leads to thoughts, words, and actions that are non-love based, they substitute the temporal for the divine. This is idolatry.

Earlier, John said believers who desire fellowship with God must walk in the light, as Jesus is the light. Here, he concludes with a warning about the lure of the world's dark forces. Next, John will address what Jesus will do to help believers who are not yet born of God stay on track for the receipt of eternal life.

The Gift of Eternal Life

Spiral Text (1:1–7; 5:18–21)

John has taken us back to his awe-inspiring witness of the resurrected Jesus when he and the other disciples fully realized Jesus was the *Word of life*—the very Word who was from the beginning with God! They heard him, saw him, and touched him, and he breathed on them to give them eternal life through the Holy Spirit.

John proclaims the eternal life and the cleansing of sin that Jesus, the *word of life* brings.

In this Part I of his three-part letter, John introduces God's New Covenant and plan for the restoration of eternal life. John takes us directly to the specifics of this good news regarding eternal life.

- He defines it—eternal life is having fellowship with the Father and his Son, which is to be in joyous communion with them.
- He identifies when access is available, which is in one's own lifetime.
- He describes what to do to receive it—walk in the light.
- He addresses the issue of sin—Jesus cleanses it.
- He describes its benefits—recipients don't lose it, don't sin (mortally), and are protected from the evil one.

You may have found this information to be new and different from what you have heard before. This is not surprising. Even by the end of the 1st century, the writers who came before John were targeting varying audiences. By the time John was writing, he assembled, clarified, and consolidated what these writers had covered into one succinct letter.

John set out to convey a precise statement of God's mission through Jesus. In essence, John wrote a tutorial to explain what writers before him had said. Now, imagine what 2,000 years of interpretation by Christianity's many different scholars and denominations has bought! There are sure to be differences, but by reading John's own words, you have the opportunity to see the source material for yourself.

John's letters actually formulate much of Christianity's foundational precepts, no matter which denomination.

- Excerpts from 1 John appear in the *Common Lectionary*.[18]
- The Catholic Catechism is full of references to 1 John.[19]
- Martin Luther called 1 John, "An outstanding epistle. It can buoy up afflicted hearts."[20]
- John Wesley stated that for many readers these epistles still ring true.[21]

So what is next? The basic presupposition that underlies all Christianity is choice. John ends Part I by instructing his community of believers to keep themselves from idols. God offers everyone the opportunity to receive eternal life now, but under the New Covenant, each person must choose to opt in. This has not changed since John and others wrote some 2,000 years ago. So let's continue on to Part II to see what those choices entail.

---

[18] C. Clifton Black, *Introduction, Commentary, and Reflections, The First, Second, and Third Letters of John, The New Interpreter's Bible Volume Twelve* (Nashville TN Abingdon Press, 1994) 377

[19] *Catechism of the Catholic Church* , Second Edition, (Libreria Editrice Vaticana, 1994, 1997)

[20] C. Clifton Black, *Introduction, Commentary, and Reflections, The First, Second, and Third Letters of John, The New Interpreter's Bible Volume Twelve* (Nashville TN Abingdon Press, 1994) 378

[21] Ibid., 378

Peter states:

"God raised him on the third day and made him manifest not to all the people but to us who were chosen by God as witnesses . . ."

—(Acts 10:40-41)

How to Receive the Gift:
Believe and Love

Part II
Believe and Love
Spiral Text (1:8–2:29; 3:11–5:17)

INTRODUCTION

In the upcoming five chapters of Part II, John will lay out the particulars of what it means to believe in Jesus and how to receive eternal life.

- **Chapter 4:** *Jesus the Advocate* answers how Jesus will support believers.
- **Chapter 5:** *The Believing Community* addresses the pivotal issue each type of believer faces.
- **Chapter 6:** *Keep His Commandment* answers how to walk as Jesus walked, how to be in the light, and how to love God.
- **Chapter 7:** *The New Commandment* addresses the two precepts of the new commandment and ways to keep them.
- **Chapter 8:** *The Reason to Love One Another and to Believe* answers: why God offered eternal life, why people should love each other, why God sent his Son, why love will reign over fear, and why faith is needed.

These chapters present a systematic explanation of Christianity's two great foundations—belief and love. We are excited to present what John says in spiral form, which is how his listeners would have comprehended it

You may find that the clarity provided by the spiral text will bring new insights that may raise questions. Please remember, you are reading John for what he, Jesus' beloved disciple had to say. We hope this will bring a greater appreciation of Christianity's roots and deeper faith.

"And this is his commandment that we should believe in the name of his Son Jesus Christ and love one another just as he has commanded us" (1 Jn 3:23).

CHAPTER 4

Jesus the Advocate
Spiral Text (1:8–2:2)

INTRODUCTION

In the prior chapter, John introduced God's plan to restore eternal life along with a summary of its magnificent benefits. He concluded with a call to stay away from the temptations (idols) of the world that would steal one's loyalty away from God. The goal is for humanity to come out of the darkness, which will require dealing with the chief obstacle to eternal life—sin.

In this chapter, John tells believers they do not have to trek on this mighty journey alone and backs it up with a breakthrough announcement of the advocacy that Jesus provides on their behalf.

- Jesus will forgive all past sins when people come to believe in his name.
- If believers confess their sins, Jesus will forgive their sins and cleanse their unrighteousness ongoing, all the way to their receipt of eternal life.

John states Jesus shepherds believers on their journey to eternal life. He is the sinner's Advocate with the Father. The term *advocate* or *counselor* is the same term used for the Holy Spirit, but in this case, John is saying Jesus is the Advocate, not the Holy Spirit. When a believer no longer sins mortally, Jesus sends the Holy Spirit to provide eternal life, guidance, and protection from that point on. This chapter brings news on two fronts.

- John identifies Jesus as the sinner's Advocate, and in so doing, John clearly differentiates between Jesus' and the Holy Spirit's advocacy.

- John states people must confess their sins to prepare themselves to live in the presence of God's pure light eternally.

SPIRAL TEXT

ORIENTATION

Read the spiral text below to get started with this chapter.

1 JOHN 1:8–2:2

Confess

[1:8a]If we say we have no sin [8c]and the truth is not in us, [8b]we deceive ourselves. [10a]If we say we have not sinned [10c]and his word is not in us, [10b]we make him a liar.

[9]If we confess our sins, he is faithful and just, and will forgive our sins and cleanse us from all unrighteousness [2:2]and he is the expiation for our sins and not for ours only but also for the sins of the whole world.

Jesus the Advocate

[2:1]My little children, I am writing this to you so that you may not sin; but if anyone does sin, we have an advocate with the Father, Jesus Christ the righteous.

COMMENTARY

CONFESS

Spiral text: [1:8a]If we say we have no sin [8c]and the truth is not in us, [8b]we deceive ourselves. [10a]If we say we have not sinned [10c]and his word is not in us, [10b]we make him a liar.

[9]If we confess our sins, he is faithful and just, and will forgive our sins and cleanse us from all unrighteousness [2:2]and he is the expiation for our sins and not for ours only but also for the sins of the whole world.

JOHN'S PURPOSE
John opens by taking us straight into the matter of sin. God sent Jesus to save the world, which is where the sin problem is.

> *For God sent the Son into the world, not to condemn the world,*
> *but that the world might be saved through him* (Jn 3:17).

John's purpose in this section of the letter is to announce Jesus' role as the believer's Advocate and explain how to receive Jesus' assistance in dealing with sin, which basically requires confession. However, before John gets to confession, he brings up two situations that would keep a believer from dealing with their sin.

TWO TRAPS THAT PRECLUDE ACCESS TO JESUS' SUPPORT
John begins by marking two serious pitfalls to which believers can succumb. Both forestall any assistance from Jesus, which precludes their being able to reach the born-of-God state. In both situations, people claim *not* to sin; yet, as John notes, because neither the truth nor the word is in them, they are *not* born of God. They are still sinning.

> *No one who abides in him sins . . .* (1 Jn 3:6).

In the first instance, people deceive themselves.

[1:8a]*If we say we have no sin* [8c]*and the truth is not in us,* [8b]*we deceive ourselves.* (1 Jn 1:8 spiral text).

These people are *not* born of God because the truth (God) is *not* in them, yet they claim *not* to sin. Therefore, their actions are not as loving as they think they are, so they deceive themselves.

THE SECOND PITFALL

In the second instance, they make Jesus a liar.

[10a]*If we say we have not sinned* [10c]*and his word is not in us,* [10b]*we make him a liar.* (1 Jn 1:10 spiral text).

John says that whoever keeps Jesus' word will be born of God and receive eternal life.

. . . whoever keeps his word . . . may be sure that we are in him (1 Jn 2:4).

Therefore, these people see Jesus as a liar because they claim they have not sinned; yet they do not have the eternal life Jesus was supposed to give. Therefore, they do not believe Jesus comes through with his promise. They see Jesus as a liar and doubt he could be the true Son of God because God is truth. Thus, they would not seek Jesus' advocacy for forgiveness either, which sabotages their chance for eternal life.

WHAT IS JOHN DOING?

In both situations, these believers put themselves in the position of not asking Jesus for his assistance, all the while, they continue to sin by not keeping the Father's commandments. Each pitfall is one of the parts of the Father's commandment.

- In the first situation, where their actions are not as loving as they think, they are violating the love part of the commandment.

- In the second situation, where they see Jesus as a liar and, therefore, not the Son of God, they are violating the belief in his name part of the commandment.

Sin is by definition always a violation of one or both parts of this commandment. Keeping the commandment is the only way to receive eternal life.

And this is his commandment, that we should believe in the name of his Son Jesus Christ and love one another, just as he has commanded us (1 Jn 3:23).

So, how do people get out of this mess?

CONFESS

John is telling his audience to look more closely at their own behavior. Both examples point to the reality that sin is in play. John is telling them that Jesus is there for them to forgive their sins, but they must initiate the process. Because they have freewill, they must ask.

They need to confess. Here is why. To confess a sin is to *stop denying it*. Confession entails:

- Recognizing the sin
- Being willing to sincerely acknowledge its harm
- Actually admitting it

WHAT IS DIFFERENT ABOUT CONFESSING TO JESUS?

A confession in a worldly setting is quite different from a confession to Jesus. Worldly justice requires punishment for wrongdoing. The goal is to balance the scales. However, a confession to Jesus elicits his merciful forgiveness. He provides the true release from the effects of sin.

Jesus offers mercy because he came to save not to condemn the world, and as John says, he is just and faithful to his mission, which means he follows the will of God completely.

If we confess our sins, he is faithful and just, and will forgive our sins and cleanse us from all unrighteousness (1 Jn 1:9).

FORGIVE AND CLEANSE
John makes an important point by indicating Jesus' two-fold response to confession. He forgives and cleanses. Forgiveness sends a sin away.

"For I will be merciful toward their iniquities, and I will remember their sins no more" (Heb 8:12).

However, sin also leaves a residual effect on the sinner, such as guilt, or a felt loss of dignity and self-esteem. Because these effects interfere with the development of a loving lifestyle, Jesus offers more than forgiveness; he also cleanses the wrongdoing, the evil, and the injustice of the sin.

JESUS' CLEANSING IS FOR THE WORLD
Since Jesus' mission is to save the world, God could have had him cleanse the sins of the whole world as a one-time mass cleansing and provide eternal life for all, but God did not. God honors humanity's freewill; his plan is for each person to choose his or her destiny. Whoever wants to join in fellowship with God can do so by choosing to live a love-based life.

He who does not love does not know God; for God is love (1 Jn 4:8).

Jesus' supreme obedience to the Father through his death and resurrection put the power of love into force—it is love that defeats death. This leaves us with an important question. Since Jesus died on the cross over 2,000 years ago, how does his cleansing activity reach those who wish to turn toward love today?

HOW TO INITIATE THE JOURNEY TO GOD
The catalyst that initiates the journey to God and provides access to Jesus' support is the decision to believe in the name of Jesus, the Son of God. By this, anyone, anywhere in the world can receive Jesus' support. It starts at a person's point of belief, when Jesus forgives all sins committed prior to that

point. This enables them to begin their journey to God with a clean slate. Next, John explains what to do about sins committed after that point.

JESUS THE ADVOCATE

> **Spiral text:** [2:1]My little children, I am writing this to you so that you may not sin; but if anyone does sin, we have an advocate with the Father, Jesus Christ the righteous.

JESUS IS THE ADVOCATE (*PARAKLETOS*)

Knowing that believers, who step on the path toward love, will take missteps along the way, John assures them they have the infinite power of Jesus to support them. Jesus is their Advocate. Jesus, who sits at God's right hand, is the believer's personal intercessor. Jesus said he would do this for those who acknowledge him.

"So everyone who acknowledges me before men, I also will acknowledge before my Father who is in heaven (Mat 10:32).

Jesus, as their Advocate (Counselor) will be with them until they are ready to receive eternal life.

The Greek word *parakletos*[22] that John uses for advocate in the passage we are considering is the same word he uses to refer to the Holy Spirit as the Counselor (Advocate) in four related passages in his Gospel. This limited and particular use of the word led us to wonder if John was suggesting the existence of two Counselors. Indeed, he is!

This is very significant because it is the first time John directly differentiates the nature of the support provided by Jesus as Counselor and that of the Holy Spirit as Counselor.

TWO PARACLETES: JESUS, THE ADVOCATE (COUNSELOR) AND THE HOLY SPIRIT, THE COUNSELOR

These two paracletes do *not* do the same things; they support believers in distinctly different ways. To understand how they are different, we will follow John's tracks through his use of the Greek word *parakletos*

---

[22] http://classic.net.bible.org/strong.php?id=3875.

- *Parakletos* appears only five times in the entire New Testament. Once in the passage we are considering of this letter, and four times in John's Gospel. All of its Gospel appearances refer to the Holy Spirit as "Counselor."
- The word *parakletos* is commonly translated as either advocate or counselor.
- The four uses of *parakletos* in John's Gospel are in Jesus' Farewell Address, and they directly relate to two questions:

  o Are there two Counselors?
  o If so, how are they different?

JESUS WILL SEND ANOTHER COUNSELOR

Parakletos appears first when Jesus tells the disciples the Father will send *another* Counselor (the Holy Spirit) to them.

> *"And I will pray the Father, and he will give you another Counselor (parakletos), to be with you forever, even the Spirit of truth, . . .* (Jn 14:16–17).

Because Jesus clearly identifies the Holy Spirit as "another" or a second Counselor, Jesus is referring to himself as the first Counselor. Another confirmation of the existence of a second Counselor comes a few verses later, when Jesus states he taught the disciples while he was still with them, but upon his leaving, the Father will send the Holy Spirit in his name.

> *"These things I have spoken to you, while I am still with you. But the Counselor (parakletos), the Holy Spirit, whom the Father will send in my name . . ."* (Jn 14:25–26).

On a third occasion, Jesus states that he initiates the sending of another Counselor who proceeds from the Father. This time, John adds new information. This Counselor (*parakletos*) will bear witness to Jesus because he has been with Jesus from the beginning.

> *"But when the Counselor comes, whom I shall send to you from the Father, even the Spirit of truth, who proceeds from the Father, he will bear witness to me;"* (Jn 15:26)

Later, Jesus tells his disciples that it is to their advantage for him to leave because without him doing so, they could not have the "second" Counselor come to them.

> *"Nevertheless I tell you the truth: it is to your advantage that I go away, for if I do not go away, the Counselor (parakletos), will not come to you; but if I go, I will send him to you"* (Jn 16:7).

WHAT IS THE ADVANTAGE?

Receipt of the Holy Spirit brings many benefits, but the crucial one is eternal life, which the Holy Spirit brings upon Jesus' discretion.

> *"And I will pray the Father, and he will give you another Counselor (parakletos), to be with you forever"* (Jn 14:16).

Jesus confirms that the granting of "another Counselor" (the Holy Spirit) is the granting of eternal life by the fact he tells the disciples this Counselor will be with them forever.

THREE PERSONS OF THE TRINITY—TWO COUNSELORS

John has identified three facilitators in God's plan; they are recognized as the three persons of the Trinity:

- God the Father who sent his Son for salvation of the world.

    > *For God sent the Son into the world . . . that the world might be saved through him* (Jn 3:17).

- God's Son, Jesus Christ, who as the first counselor, forgives sins and grants eternal life.

    > *And the blood of Jesus cleanses us from all sin* (1 Jn 1:7b).

> *"And I know that his commandment is eternal life"* (Jn 12:50a).

- The Holy Spirit who, as the second Counselor, brings eternal life and ongoing protection to those whom Jesus designates.

> *"If you love me, you will keep my commandments. And I will pray the Father, and he will give you another Counselor to be with you forever"* (Jn 14:15–16).

> *"He on whom you see the Spirit descend and remain, this is he who baptizes with the Holy Spirit"'* (Jn 1:33c).

WHAT THE DISCIPLES RECEIVED

While no one since Jesus' disciples will have the opportunity to be physically with him for in-person forgiveness and support, they will be able to receive the ongoing support of his forgiveness of sin, his cleansing, and his granting of eternal life through his "first" Counselor functions. This is clearly God's plan. Let's look at the references from John's Gospel that support this.

First, John tells us the disciples received the Holy Spirit (eternal life) in their lifetime.

> *Jesus said to them again, "Peace be with you"* . . . *And when he had said this, he breathed on them, and said to them, "Receive the Holy Spirit"* (Jn 20:21–22).

This is when the disciples were protected from the evil one for the remainder of their life on earth and forever.

> *"I do not pray that thou shouldst take them out of the world, but that thou shouldst keep them from the evil one"* (Jn 17:15).

Next, Jesus extends the same benefits of eternal life and protection from evil for all who believe (follow his commandments) through the word of the disciples.

"I do not pray for these only, but also for those who believe in me through their word, that they may all be one . . . that they also may be in us, so that the world may believe that thou hast sent me" (Jn 17:20–21).

John differentiates between Jesus and the Holy Spirit as Counselors in order to align with the two phases of a believer's life with God.

> **Phase one:** Being en route to receiving eternal life.
> **Phase two:** Having received eternal life (becoming born of God).

John passionately encourages his audience to do as we titled this book—to seize life (with God) now! As a disciple who received eternal life, John knows the joy of fellowship with God, and he knows that those he addresses have the opportunity to receive it during their life on earth, which is as true for you, the modern reader, as it was for the audience John addressed in his day.

CONCLUSION

In Part I of this letter, John announced the restoration of eternal life. In this chapter, John launches Part II by identifying Jesus' crucial role as the believer's Advocate. Jesus will provide forgiveness of their sins and cleansing, if believers ask him to.

John initiates his discussion of this matter with the core reason believers would *not* go to Jesus for his support. It is their denial about their sinning. This is so significant that if they succumb to the two pitfalls John describes, they will not receive eternal life. However, John assures his audience that Jesus is faithful and just, and that they must confess their sins in order to walk in the light.

Next, John will address the believing community to make recommendations that are specific to believers who are in different stages of their journey.

CHAPTER 5

The Believing Community
Spiral Text (2:12–2:28)

INTRODUCTION

In his Gospel, John's purpose was to enable people to believe in Jesus' name, but in this letter his purpose is to help believers receive eternal life. In this chapter, John tailors his remarks to specific types of believers who have or have not received eternal life. If you are or have been a Christian, you will find yourself amongst them. There are believers who:

- Have completed the journey to eternal life and are living it now
- Have not yet been born of God so they are still developing their ability to live from loving intentions
- Have fallen away

John offers advice, encouragement, and warnings to shed light on issues that matter to each type of believer. He pinpoints what to do and what *not* to do to achieve his vision of all believers being able to gladly and confidently anticipate Jesus' second coming.

The key to understanding this chapter is to know who John is addressing at any point in the text, which is quite obscure in the linear text. However, the spiral text clears this up. We will provide headlines and comments to mark John's focus throughout.

SPIRAL TEXT

ORIENTATION

Read the spiral text below to start your consideration of this chapter.

1 JOHN 2:12–2:28

To the Entire Believing Community

[2:12]I am writing to you, little children, because your sins are forgiven for his sake. [2:28]And now, little children, abide in him, so that when he appears we may have confidence and not shrink from him in shame at his coming.

To Believers Who Are Born of God

[2:13a]I am writing to you, fathers, because you know him who is from the beginning. [14a]I write to you, fathers, because you know him who is from the beginning.

[13b]I am writing to you, young men, because you have overcome the evil one. [14b]I write to you, young men, because you are strong, [14d]and you have overcome the evil one, [14c]and the word of God abides in you.

[13c]And I write to you, children, because you know the Father. [2:27a]As for you, the anointing which you received from him abides in you; [2:27e]abide in him. [2:27b]And you have no need that any one should teach you; as his anointing teaches you about everything, [2:27d]and just as it has taught you, [2:27c]is true and is no lie.

To Believers Who Are Not Yet Born of God

[2:15a]Do not love the world or the things in the world. [16a]For all that is in the world [16c]is not of the Father, but is of the world: [16b]lust of the flesh and lust of the eyes and the pride of life. [15b]If anyone loves the world, love for the Father is not in him. [17]The world passes away, and the lust in it; but he who does the will of God abides forever.

2:24Let what you heard from the beginning abide in you. If what you heard from the beginning abides in you, then you will abide in the Son and in the Father. 25And this is what he has promised us, eternal life. 26I write this to you about those who would deceive you.

Believers Who No Longer Believe—the Antichrists

2:18Children, it is the last hour and as you have heard that antichrist is coming, so now many antichrists have come therefore we know that it is the last hour.

19aThey went out from us, but they were not of us; 19cbut they went out, that it might be plain that they all are not of us; 19bfor if they had been of us, they would have continued with us.

2:22aWho is the liar but he who denies that Jesus is the Christ? 23No one who denies the Son has the Father. He who confesses the Son has the Father also. 22bThis is the antichrist, he who denies the Father and the Son.

To Believers Born of God—Let the Antichrists Go

2:20But you have been anointed by the Holy One, and you all know. 21b You know that no lie comes from the truth. 21aI write to you, not because you do not know the truth, but because you know it.

COMMENTARY

TO THE ENTIRE BELIEVING COMMUNITY

> **Spiral text:** [2:12]I am writing to you, little children, because your sins are forgiven for his sake. [2:28]And now, little children, abide in him, so that when he appears we may have confidence and not shrink from him in shame at his coming.

ALL PAST SINS ARE FORGIVEN

John indicates he writes to believers when he says his audience has had their sins forgiven for Jesus' sake. The term *for his sake* refers to what Jesus did that led to the forgiveness of sins—his demonstration of supreme love and obedience to the Father during his Passion. Jesus' forgiveness is activated at the point people believe in his name.

> *. . . And the blood of Jesus his Son cleanses us from all sin* (1 Jn 1:7c).

HOW DOES ONE ABIDE IN HIM?

Love is what puts believers on the road to eternal life.

> *For this is the message, which you have heard from the beginning, that we should love one another,* (1 Jn 3:11)

> *If what you heard from the beginning abides in you, then you will abide in the Son and in the Father. And this is what he has promised us, eternal life* (1 Jn 2:24b–25).

John drives home his point by stating the outcome he desires for every believer—to anticipate Jesus' coming again with glad and bold confidence.

To Believers Who Are Born of God

> **Spiral text:** [2:13a]I am writing to you, fathers, because you know him who is from the beginning. [14a]I write to you, fathers, because you know him who is from the beginning.
>
> [2:13b]I am writing to you, young men, because you have overcome the evil one. [14b]I write to you, young men, because you are strong, [14d]and you have overcome the evil one, [14c]and the word of God abides in you.
>
> [13c]And I write to you, children, because you know the Father. [2:27a]As for you, the anointing which you received from him abides in you; [2:27e]abide in him. [2:27b]And you have no need that any one should teach you; as his anointing teaches you about everything, [2:27d]and just as it has taught you, [2:27c]is true and is no lie.

Who Are Born of God?

John classifies those who are born of God into two categories: the fathers and the young men. John does not mention women, but they are also included.

- The fathers represent the group who knew or saw Jesus when he walked the earth to launch God's plan for eternal life.
- The young men are *not* old enough to have seen Jesus. They received eternal life because they have the strength of faith. This is John's call to faith to all believers.

   . . . and this is the victory that overcomes the world, our faith (5:4b).

They "know" God

How do we know that these fathers and young men are born of God? John states that they *know* the Father. The Greek word know *ginosko*[23] is the

---

[23] http://classic.net.bible.org/strong.php?id=1097.

word he uses consistently when he refers to having eternal life. John describes their born-of-God state three ways.

- They have overcome the evil one.
- The word of God abides in them.
- The anointing they received from God abides in them.

No matter how they got there, whether by sight or by faith, they have done it! They have overcome evil to receive eternal life. John reminds them to abide in Him, not that John is suggesting they are at risk of losing God's Spirit. Once granted it will never be revoked. John's purpose is to encourage them to be confident that they are ongoing beneficiaries of God's truth.

To Believers Who Are Not Yet Born of God

Spiral text: 2:15aDo not love the world or the things in the world. 16aFor all that is in the world, 16cis not of the Father, 16bbut is of the world, lust of the flesh and lust of the eyes and the pride of life. 15bIf anyone loves the world, love for the Father is not in him. 17The world passes away, and the lust in it; but he who does the will of God abides forever.

2:24Let what you heard from the beginning abide in you. If what you heard from the beginning abides in you, then you will abide in the Son and in the Father. 25And this is what he has promised us, eternal life. 26I write this to you about those who would deceive you.

WHAT TO NOT LOVE
John has already urged believers to stay away from idols. Here, he warns them of three areas ripe for idolatry.

- **Lust of the flesh**—represents all cravings/desires that feed the physical nature of a human as opposed to spiritual nature.

    Jesus answered, "Truly, truly, I say to you, unless one is born of water and the Spirit, he cannot enter the kingdom

> *of God. That which is born of the flesh is flesh, and that which is born of the Spirit is spirit"* (Jn 3:5–6).

- **Lust of the eyes**—represents all the desires generated from what one sees. Physical sight sees only the visible, whereas spiritual sight, which is where truth lies, is invisible and invincible.

  > *Jesus said . . . "I came into this world, that those who do not see may see, and that those who see may become blind"* (Jn 9:39).

- **Pride of life**—(The Greek word for life is *bios*[24] means biological life, which refers to worldly life). Pride implies which always refers to God's life or eternal life). Pride is more than boastful talk or excessive focus on worldly wealth, goods, and accomplishments. A person with pride thinks he or she can be self-sufficient without God, as Adam and Eve did.

John punctuates these choices with the clear divide of life and death—those who succumb to their lure remain of the world, and like the world, they too will pass away. Those who love the Father and do his will, stay with him forever. How do we know what the Father's will is?

LOVE ONE ANOTHER
The Father's will is what they heard from the beginning.

> *For this is the message, which you have heard from the beginning, that we should love one another* (1 Jn 3:11).

In contradiction to the Father's command to love, there are people who deliberately try to deceive. Because those who are still en route to eternal life are particularly vulnerable, John tells this group to hang on to God's simple precept—abide in love because with it, they will abide forever.

---

[24] http://classic.net.bible.org/strong.php?id=979.

BELIEVERS WHO NO LONGER BELIEVE—THE ANTICHRISTS

Spiral text: [18]Children, it is the last hour and as you have heard that antichrist is coming, so now many antichrists have come therefore we know that it is the last hour.

[2:19a]They went out from us, but they were not of us; [19c]but they went out, that it might be plain that they all are not of us; [19b]for if they had been of us, they would have continued with us.

[2:22a]Who is the liar but he who denies that Jesus is the Christ? [23]No one who denies the Son has the Father. He who confesses the Son has the Father also. [22b]This is the antichrist, he who denies the Father and the Son.

THE ANTICHRISTS ARE AGAINST CHRIST

John addresses those who are born of God to tell them the last hour is upon them because many antichrists are arriving on the scene. Who are these antichrists? Only John uses this term; so let's look at the point he wishes to make by it.

Antichrists are people who once believed in Jesus Christ, who now deny him. They stand in opposition to two aspects of Jesus incarnate: to him as the Christ and to him as the Son of God. The logic of why this is a problem goes like this:

When they deny Jesus is the Christ, they deny that he is the Savior, the Messiah.

This denial means they deny that God sent his Son to save the world, which means they deny the Son's incarnation.

Therefore, they deny Jesus is the Son of God.

Denial of Jesus as God's Son is ultimately a denial of the Father.

Since God is Truth, those who deny Christ are liars.

WHAT ARE THE RAMIFICATIONS OF DENYING CHRIST?

Those who fail to believe in Jesus as the Son of God will not get to first base in coming into fellowship with God. They simply will not receive eternal life.

> *"For this is the will of the Father, that everyone who sees the Son and believes in him should have eternal life; and I will raise him up at the last day"* (Jn 6:40).

Jesus is the way to eternal life.

> . . . *"I am the way, and the truth, and the life; no one comes to the Father, but by me"* (Jn 14:6).

Jesus is the one who forgives sin and cleanses unrighteousness; both are necessary to live a life of loving one another. However, the antichrists who do not believe in Jesus would have no reason to go to him to cleanse their sin; therefore, eternal life will not be theirs.

> *"If I had not come and spoken to them, they would not have sin; but now they have no excuse for their sin. He who hates me hates my Father also"* (Jn 15:22–23).

TO BELIEVERS BORN OF GOD—LET THE ANTICHRISTS GO

> **Spiral text:** [2:20]But you have been anointed by the Holy One, and you all know. [21b]You know that no lie comes from the truth. [21a]I write to you, not because you do not know the truth, but because you know it.

YOU KNOW THE TRUTH

John makes a straightforward, non-judgmental assessment of the situation. Those who chose to leave did not really believe the truth to begin with. The thing for believers to focus on is the truth, not these liars.

John affirms that those who are born of God know the truth; the Holy Spirit has anointed them. John stresses they know the capital "T"

Truth—they *know* God. How can they be sure that they know? John answers this in the next chapter.

CONCLUSION

In a clear, logical dissertation, which you could call a pep talk, John tells his community of believers what to keep their focus on. He tailors his remarks to two categories of believers:

- Those anointed by the Holy Spirit, who have received eternal life
- Those who are striving toward that end

Bottom line, both sets of believers should abide in him (Jesus' love). The anointed believers are *not* at risk of losing eternal life; however, by staying focused on abiding in him, they will more fully realize the presence of the Holy Spirit they have received.

As for those who are on the journey to eternal life, John tells them to avoid lust and pride. As John sees it, either these believers are "on" with God or they are not. If they choose to love the world, they will pass away along with its idols, but if they choose God, they will abide with him forever.

John tells all believers the hour for Jesus' return is near. John's orientation to the antichrists who have come on the scene is consistent with his advice about the worldly. Do not pay attention to them and their deadly lures, but stay focused on the truth.

What John says in this chapter is as relevant for every type of believer today as it was 2,000 years ago. John provides a beautiful opportunity for every reader to make a personal assessment of where he or she is on the path to joining God's eternal loving presence.

CHAPTER 6

Keep His Commandments
Spiral Text (2:3–11)

INTRODUCTION

John will summarize everything he said so far into one key piece of advice—keep God's commandments. When believers do this consistently, they will know for sure they have eternal life. They will be in the light and have no cause for worries about stumbling. When their love of God reaches "perfection," leaving them with no fear of the future of Jesus' coming, their Judgment Day will, in essence, have arrived.

John assures his audience the darkness of the world is falling away and the light is already shining. He leaves them with the promise that he will write an update to the old commandment to reflect God's magnificent gift of eternal life to the world. . John answers the following six important questions in this brief chapter.

1. How to be assured of receiving eternal life
2. How to be in the light
3. How to walk as Jesus walked
4. How to love God
5. How to have confidence on Judgment Day
6. How to please God

SPIRAL TEXT

ORIENTATION
Read the spiral text below to start your consideration of the text in this chapter.

1 JOHN 2:3–11

Walk in the Light—Keep His Commandments & Love Your Brother

2:3And by this we may be sure that we know him, if we keep his commandments. 5Whoever keeps his word, in him truly love for God is perfected. By this we may be sure that we are in him.

2:4He who says, "I know him" but disobeys his commandments, is a liar, and the truth is not in him; 6He who says he abides in him ought to walk in the same way in which he walked. 9He who says he is in the light and hates his brother is in the darkness still. 11He who hates his brother is in the darkness and walks in the darkness, and does not know where he is going, because the darkness has blinded his eyes.

2:10He who loves his brother abides in the light, and in it there is no cause for stumbling.

The True Light and a New Commandment

2:7aBeloved, I am writing you no new commandment, but an old commandment, which you had from the beginning. 8aYet I am writing you a new commandment, which is true in him and in you. 8cThe true light is already shining 8bbecause the darkness is passing away. 2:7bThe old commandment is the word, which you have heard.

COMMENTARY

WALK IN THE LIGHT—KEEP HIS COMMANDMENTS AND LOVE YOUR BROTHER

Spiral text: [2:3] And by this we may be sure that we know him, if we keep his commandments. [5] Whoever keeps his word, in him truly love for God is perfected by this we may be sure that we are in him.

[2:4] He who says, "I know him" but disobeys his commandments, is a liar, and the truth is not in him; [6] He who says he abides in him ought to walk in the same way in which he walked. [9] He who says he is in the light and hates his brother is in the darkness still. [11] He who hates his brother is in the darkness and walks in the darkness, and does not know where he is going, because the darkness has blinded his eyes.

[10] He who loves his brother abides in the light, and in it there is no cause for stumbling.

JOHN'S SINGULAR RESPONSE TO HOW TO BE SURE

John has just told his audience what it takes to be born of God. Here, he deals with how they can be sure that they are. He communicates the answer by returning to the born-of-God theme with four memory-locking repetitions of the phrase *in him*.

- We are *in him*.
- *In him*, love for God is perfected.
- Truth *in him*.
- Abide *in him*.

There is one fundamental answer to the question of how to be sure; it is to keep God's commandments. John conveys this answer when he makes the following three statements:

- Keep his commandments.

- Keep his word.
- Walk as Jesus walked.

With this said, let us look at what John suggests about how to keep God's commandments.

THE KEY TO SUCCESS

John uses the Greek word *tereo*[25] when he advises his audience to keep God's commandments and keep his word. The translation of this word can be either to *obey* or to *keep*. We prefer the translation *to keep* because the basic idea of this word is to hold the commandments in view by paying careful attention to them. Eternal life does not arrive because of occasional acts of obedience; what counts is the consistency.

> ... *"but I do know him and I <u>keep</u> (tereo) his word"* (Jn 8:55).

To walk as Jesus walked as John advises, is not a one-time event; it is durational. The term *walk* is a Hebrew idiom for living.[26] Therefore, to walk like Jesus is to live like Jesus, which is to please the Father all the time.

> ... *"I always do what is pleasing to him"* (Jn 8:29).

What does one do to please God? The answer is to love God by keeping his commandments.

> *For this is the love of God that we keep his commandments* (1 Jn 5:3).

When people consistently keep God's commandments, their love for God *is perfected*—it is complete.

> *In this is love perfected with us, that we may have confidence for the day of judgment, because as he is so are we in this world* (1 Jn 4:17).

---

[25] http://classic.net.bible.org/verse.php?book=Joh&chapter=14&verse=15.
[26] http://classic.net.bible.org/strong.php?id=4043.

When this occurs, they will be born of God, which brings assurance of eternal life. They will abide in God permanently and will have no reason to fear Judgment Day because it will have, in essence, occurred.

CHOICE POINTS

John uses contrast to focus our attention on life's choice points. He packs verses 2:9–11, with five statements that compare what happens when one keeps the Father's commandments and what happens when one does not.

TABLE 6-1. CONTRASTING EFFECTS OF BEING AND NOT BEING BORN OF GOD

#	WHAT <u>NOT</u> BEING BORN OF GOD LOOKS LIKE	WHAT BEING BORN OF GOD LOOKS LIKE
1.	Disobeys his commandments	Keeps his commandments
2.	People lie	Truth is in you
3.	To be blinded by darkness	To be in the light
4.	To hate a brother	To love a brother
5.	To stumble	To know where you are going

Why is John making such a strong pitch to keep God's commandments in this chapter? He is getting us ready for the announcement of a new commandment. When he describes it in the next chapter, he will build on these contrasting choice points to explain the meaning of its terms and its effects.

The True Light and a New Commandment

Spiral text: [2:7a]Beloved, I am writing you no new commandment, but an old commandment, which you had from the beginning. [8a]Yet I am writing you a new commandment, which is true in him and in you. [8c]The true light is already shining [8b]~~because~~ the darkness is passing away. [2:7b]The old commandment is the word, which you have heard.

The old commandment

John is not speaking in riddles when he says he is and is not writing a new commandment. He is going to do both. He will expand the old commandment because something so significant has occurred that it calls for an update. Therefore, the commandment John will announce is both new and old. Let's look at the old commandment; then go to the reason for the update.

> *For this is the message, which you have heard from the beginning, that we should love one another* (1 Jn 3:11).

Jesus carried the Father's commandment to love forward on many occasions. For example, he did it in his Farewell Address when he told his disciples to love one another.

> *"This is my commandment, that you love one another as I have loved you"* (Jn 15:12).

> *"This I command you, to love one another"* (Jn 15:17).

The reason for a new commandment

Jesus' coming in human form is the reason for a new commandment. He is the true light that is already shining. Those who believe in him as the Son of God have access to his light of life. Their darkness can depart because they have the opportunity to receive God's gift of eternal life.

Again Jesus spoke to them, saying, "I am the light of the world.
The one who follows me will never walk in darkness, but will have
the light of life" (Jn 8:12).

Jesus brings hope that did not exist before his arrival. He not only grants eternal life but through his cleansing of sin, he makes it possible for humankind to live a love-based life. John will have more to say about the keeping of the "old" commandment to love in the next chapter.

CHAPTER 7

The New Commandment: Believe and Love

Spiral Text (3:11–4:6; 5:14–17)

INTRODUCTION

PREVIEW
John unveils the Father's new commandment, complete with explicit advice and tests regarding keeping its two foundational elements: to believe in Jesus' name and to love one another. John knows without a doubt keeping the commandment's two precepts will lead to eternal life.

WHAT TO LOOK FOR IN YOUR READING
Here are four points that warrant your special attention.

1. The need for the deed when it comes to loving one another.
2. The correct understanding of who Jesus is.
3. The two parts of God's new commandment and what keeping them brings.
4. Under what conditions those who are born of God may use the new Ask and Receive gift.

SPIRAL TEXT

ORIENTATION

Read the spiral text below to start your consideration of the text in this chapter.

1 JOHN 3:11–4:6; 5:14–17

Love One Another

³:¹¹For this is the message, which you have heard from the beginning that we should love one another, ¹²and not be like Cain who was of the evil one and murdered his brother. And why did he murder him? Because his own deeds were evil and his brother's righteous. ¹⁵Anyone who hates his brother is a murderer, and you know that no murderer has eternal life abiding in him.

³:¹⁷If anyone has the world's goods and sees his brother in need, yet closes his heart against him, how does God's love abide in him? ¹⁸Little children, let us not love in word or speech but in deed and in truth. ¹⁶By this we know love that he laid down his life for us; and we ought to lay down our lives for the brethren.

Love and Eternal Life

³:¹³Do not wonder, brethren, that the world hates you. ¹⁴ᵇHe who does not love abides in death. ¹⁴ᵃWe know that we have passed out of death into life, because we love the brethren. ³:²⁴ᵇAnd by this we know that he abides in us, by the Spirit, which he has given us.

The Spirit of Truth and the Spirit of Error

⁴:⁶ᵇBy this we know the spirit of truth and the spirit of error: ⁴:¹Beloved don't believe every spirit, but test the spirits to see whether they are of God; for many false prophets have gone out into the world. ⁴:⁵They are of the world, therefore what they say is of the world, and the world listens to

them. ^{6a}We are of God. Whoever knows God listens to us, and he who is not of God does not listen to us.

^{4:2}By this you know the Spirit of God: every spirit, which confesses that Jesus Christ has come in the flesh is of God, ³and every spirit, which does not confess Jesus is not of God. This is the spirit of antichrist, of which you heard that it was coming, and now it is in the world already.

^{4:4}Little children, you are of God, and have overcome them; for he who is in you is greater than he who is in the world.

The New Commandment

^{3:19a}By this we shall know that we are of the truth, ^{22b}because we keep his commandments and do what pleases him. ^{24a}All who keep his commandments abide in him, and he in them. ^{3:23}And this is his commandment: that we should believe in the name of his Son Jesus Christ and love one another, just as he has commanded us.

Ask and Receive

^{3:19b}Reassure our hearts before him ²⁰whenever our hearts condemn us; for God is greater than our hearts, and he knows everything, ^{22a}and we receive from him whatever we ask. ²¹Beloved, if our hearts do not condemn us, we have confidence before God, ^{22a}and we receive from him whatever we ask.^{5:14}And this is the confidence, which we have in him, that if we ask anything according to his will he hears us. ^{5:15}And if we know that he hears us in whatever we ask, we know that we have obtained the requests made of him.

^{5:16a}If any one sees his brother committing what is not a mortal sin (^{16c}there is sin which is mortal), I do not say that one is to pray ¹⁷for that. All wrongdoing is sin, but there is sin, which is not mortal. ^{16b}He will ask, and God will give him life for those whose sin is not mortal.

COMMENTARY

LOVE ONE ANOTHER

Spiral text: [3:11]For this is the message, which you have heard from the beginning that we should love one another [12]and not be like Cain who was of the evil one and murdered his brother. And why did he murder him? Because his own deeds were evil and his brother's righteous. [15]Anyone who hates his brother is a murderer, and you know that no murderer has eternal life abiding in him.

[3:17]If anyone has the world's goods and sees his brother in need, yet closes his heart against him, how does God's love abide in him? [18]Little children, let us not love in word or speech but in deed and in truth. [16]By this we know love that he laid down his life for us; and we ought to lay down our lives for the brethren.

THE COMMAND IS TO LOVE

Why would John use the story of Cain, who murdered his brother, to convey his message about loving one another? While this Genesis story certainly confirms that God's desire for us to love one another has been true from the beginning, John has another point to make.

Let's pick up with Cain after he and his brother made their offering to God. God looked with favor on Abel, but not on Cain. When God saw Cain's anger over this, he told Cain *if* he did what was right, he (God) would accept him. If he did not, sin would be crouching at his door.

> *The LORD said to Cain, "Why are you so angry . . . sin is crouching at your door; its desire is for you, but you must master it"* (Gen 4:6a–7).

Cain did not overcome his anger; instead, he invited his brother to the field and killed him. This story replays what happened with Adam and Eve, when evil (sin) crouched snakelike and its evil grabbed hold of them. John's point is sin and death wait for everyone who renounces love.

LOVE IN DEED AND TRUTH

Having positioned murder as evil, John takes up two more situations that preclude eternal life. When compared to murder, the two hypothetical situations, hating a brother and closing one's heart to a brother in need, do not sound so bad. However, John goes so far as to say hate is as bad as murder.

The problem with hatred and other similar thoughts is they close a person's heart to love, which blocks his or her ability to do loving deeds. This makes having non-loving thoughts as bad as doing a non-loving deed. Having a loving thought or saying a loving word is a start toward love, but they are not the real deal. To count, John is saying thoughts need to be actualized as loving deeds. The scholar Raymond Brown posits that the phrase "in deed and in truth" conveys God's plan for Christians to express the divine love that abides within them outwardly in the way they live.[27]

JESUS DEMONSTRATES WHAT LOVE IS

John hones in on Jesus' laying down his own life as the ultimate demonstration of what Christian love is. Such a love begins when people who of their freewill choose to live by love. Even Jesus indicates his will is involved in choosing to lay down his life, when he says he does so of his own accord.

> ... *"I lay down my life ... No one takes it from me, but I lay it down of my own accord"* (Jn 10:17–18a).

When John says believers ought to lay down their lives for a brother/sister, he issues an example of Christian love in action that is in contrast to worldly hatred and murder.

---

[27] Raymond E. Brown, Translation with Introduction, Notes, and Commentary, *The Anchor Bible: The Epistles of John* (New York: Doubleday, 1982) 452.

LOVE AND ETERNAL LIFE

> **Spiral text:** [3:13]Do not wonder, brethren, that the world hates you. [14b]He who does not love abides in death. [14a]We know that we have passed out of death into life, because we love the brethren. [3:24b]And by this we know that he abides in us, by the Spirit, which he has given us.

JOHN TESTIFIES TO LOVE

Having defined Christian love as true deeds that are expressed beyond words, John testifies that love is <u>the</u> means to eternal life. He presents a clear choice—love of brethren leads to life; hatred leads to death.

But even when life and death consequences are at stake, John tells his audience of believers not to be surprised that people of the world thrust their hatred upon them. He explained why in the Nicodemus story. Everyone who does evil hates the light because the light exposes the evil deeds that will lead to death.

> *For every one who does evil hates the light and does not come to the light, lest his deeds should be exposed. But he who does what is true comes to the light...* (Jn 3:20–21a).

John substantiates the efficacy of love by the fact he and the disciples were the beneficiaries of God's Spirit and great gift of eternal life because they loved the brethren as Jesus commanded.

> *... he breathed on them, and said to them. "Receive the Holy Spirit"* (Jn 20:22).

This receipt of the Holy Spirit enables John to explain the difference between the spirit of truth and the spirit of error with upmost authority.

THE SPIRIT OF TRUTH AND THE SPIRIT OF ERROR

> **Spiral text:** [4:6b]By this we know the spirit of truth and the spirit of error: [4:1]Beloved don't believe every spirit, but test the spirits to see whether they are of God, for many false prophets have gone out into the world. [5]They are of the world, therefore what they say is of the world, and the world listens to them. [4:6a]We are of God. Whoever knows God listens to us, and he who is not of God does not listen to us.
>
> [4:2] By this you know the Spirit of God: every spirit, which confesses that Jesus Christ has come in the flesh is of God, [3]and every spirit which does not confess Jesus is not of God. This is the spirit of antichrist, of which you heard that it was coming, and now it is in the world already
>
> [4:4]Little children, you are of God and have overcome them, for he who is in you is greater than he who is in the world.

WHO IS JESUS?

John was quite concerned that believers hold the correct understanding of Jesus. There are three ways to think about him; only the first is correct.

1. He is simultaneously human and divine—the correct view.
2. He is *not* divine; he is only human.
3. He is *not* human; he is only divine.

According to scholar Judith Lieu, early tradition described John as battling against the incorrect views.[28]

TWO KINDS OF ANTICHRISTS

John tells his audience the spirit of error actually exists and warns them to test the spirits of those who approach them. He has mentioned the antichrists before. They were the ones who left the community because they did not believe Jesus who came in the flesh was the Christ and the Son of God.

---

[28] Judith Lieu, *I, II & III John: A Commentary, The New Testament Library* (Louisville, KY: Westminster John Knox Press, 2008) 135–136.

However, the false prophets John refers to here are different and much more dangerous because they will try to persuade people to believe a completely false opinion of Jesus. The Apostle Paul had this to say about these false prophets.

> *But I am afraid that as the serpent deceived Eve . . . your thoughts will be led astray from a sincere and pure devotion to Christ . . . For such men are false apostles, deceitful workmen, disguising themselves as apostles of Christ* (2 Cor. 11:3; 13).

HOW TO TEST THE SPIRITS

The way to test a spirit is to find out what a person believes about Jesus. There are two incorrect views.

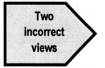

1. Jesus is not the Christ and is not the Son of God. He is **human *not* divine**.

2. Jesus is **purely divine and *not* human**.

Those who have not yet been born of God could be particularly vulnerable to being swayed by false prophets. In his second letter, John urges them to be careful so as not to lose the progress they have made.

> *Look to yourselves, that you may not lose what you have worked for, but may win a full reward* (2Jn 1:8).

There is one correct view of who Jesus is.

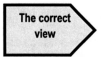

Jesus is the Christ, the Son of God. He is **divine and human**.

Those who are born of God have the correct view of Jesus. It is rock solid because God protects them from the evil one, but even so, John reminds them that God's greatness within them exceeds that of anyone who is of the world.

THE NEW COMMANDMENT

> **Spiral text:** [3:19]By this we shall know that we are of the truth, [22b]because we keep his commandments and do what pleases him. [24]All who keep his commandments abide in him, and he in them. [23]And this is his commandment: that we should believe in the name of his Son Jesus Christ and love one another, just as he has commanded us.

GOD'S NEW COMMANDMENT

John makes it official. This is where he defines the commandment that will enable all who keep it to receive eternal life. All of God's prior commandments are rolled into this new two-fold commandment.

> . . . *Believe in the name of his Son Jesus Christ and love one another, just as he has commanded us* (3:23).

Keeping this commandment is doing what pleases God. It brings the assurance of eternal life, which according to John, can begin in the here and now of this lifetime!

TO ABIDE IN GOD IS TO KNOW GOD

John says that because God is love, knowing God requires being in a state of love. Therefore, following God's command to love by doing loving deeds, is *not* a means to earn your way to God; it is the way to *know* God. Only when you are experiencing love, can you be abiding in God and God in you.

> . . . *love is of God and he who loves is born of God and knows God* (1 Jn 4:7b).

> . . . *God is love, and he who abides in love abides in God, and God abides in him.* (1 Jn 4:16).

The scholar Raymond Brown explains the logic of how following God's commandments leads to a union with God's love.

The logic is that keeping the commandments constitutes a union of the Christian's will with God's will and thus removes any obstacle to mutual love.[29]

Next, John takes up a special form of prayer that is for those who abide in God. This prayer is the way people who are in this kind of direct communion with God can properly ask for something and know God hears them and will respond.

ASK AND RECEIVE

Spiral text: [3:19b]Reassure our hearts before him [20]whenever our hearts condemn us; for God is greater than our hearts, and he knows everything, [22a]and we receive from him whatever we ask. [21]Beloved, if our hearts do not condemn us, we have confidence before God, [22a]and we receive from him whatever we ask.[5:14]And this is the confidence, which we have in him, that if we ask anything according to his will he hears us. [5:15]And if we know that he hears us in whatever we ask, we know that we have obtained the requests made of him.

[5:16a]If any one sees his brother committing what is not a mortal sin ([16c]there is sin which is mortal), I do not say that one is to pray for that. [17]All wrongdoing is sin, but there is sin, which is not mortal. [16b]He will ask, and God will give him life for those whose sin is not mortal.

JOHN ANNOUNCES A NEW FORM OF PRAYER

Those who are born of God can freely and unreservedly make requests of God and be confident they will receive what they ask for! There are two conditions necessary to activate this prayer.

1. The request must be according to God's will. If it is, God will attend to it and grant what he hears.
2. Those who activate the prayer must be free of all sin.

---

[29] Raymond E. Brown, Translation with Introduction, Notes, and Commentary, *The Anchor Bible: The Epistles of John* (New York: Doubleday, 1982) 482.

If I had cherished iniquity in my heart, the Lord would not have listened (Ps 66:18).

Even though John addresses those who are born of God, many of them realize they are *not* free of all sin, which could even lead them to wonder about their born-of-God status. John assures them that God is greater than their hearts; God knows his children. The questions we pose below will help unravel the issue of sin and its impact on the Ask and Receive prayer.

1. Do children of God still sin? Earlier, John indicated that they do not, however this does not explain why these people think they do.

    ... 3:9c and he cannot sin because he is born of God; 9b for God's nature abides in him ... (1 Jn 3:9c and b spiral text).

2. Is the concern that these children of God could lose their born-of-God status valid? The answer is no.

    He who was born of God keeps him, and the evil one does not touch him (1 Jn 5:18).

3. Do those who are born of God sin? The answer is "yes." They do sin, but it is *not* the kind of mortal sin that would preclude someone from receiving eternal life. John's example of observing a brother who is born of God committing a non-mortal sin indicates what is going on. Let's look more closely at the two types of sin and their ramifications.

MORTAL AND NON-MORTAL SIN

The difference between mortal and not-mortal sin:

*   **Mortal Sin** is the deliberate and severe violation of the love and/or belief components of the Father's commandment. It leads to permanent death. To reverse it, the individuals

must choose to correct these actions through their own freewill.

- **Non-mortal Sin** is a less severe or unintentional violation of the Father's commandment. It does *not* lead to permanent death.

People who are born of God do still commit non-mortal sins, and they need to deal with these sins. Jesus referred to this issue when he told his disciples that brothers need to wash each other's feet. He said they (the disciples) are "clean" and do not need to wash, meaning overall, they are steeped in a love-based lifestyle, but their feet will collect road dust (sin). This metaphor refers to the accumulation of non-mortal sins precipitated by walking on the dusty road of life.

> *Jesus said to him (Peter), "He who has bathed does not need to wash, except for his feet . . . If I then, your Lord and Teacher, have washed your feet, you also ought to wash one another's feet"* (Jn 13:10a; 13:15b).

Those who are born of God need be cleansed of their non-mortal sins for the good of their own countenance and to be able to use the Ask and Receive prayer. In addition to their confessing their non-mortal sins to Jesus directly, there is another way for those who are born of God to receive forgiveness of these sins. It can come by way of a brother who invokes the Ask and Receive prayer for their forgiveness. When their sins are forgiven, John says God will give them "life." Let's look at the implications of this.

WHAT DOES JOHN MEAN BY GIVING "LIFE" TO A BROTHER?

When John says that God will give life to the brother whose non-mortal sins are forgiven, it is puzzling. This brother has already received assurance of eternal life, which he cannot lose. So what is the "life" that God will give him? To understand, look at non-mortal sins as road dust that accumulates to shroud the brother's light.

Life, in this case, is a touch-up to the brother's light-filled life on earth. If a brother is observed committing one sin, it would be hard to imagine that it is the only one. So if the brother has been accumulating other sins on his walk on life's dusty roads, the Ask and Receive prayer automatically removes the whole shroud that dims his light. The prayer will not only lead to forgiveness of the sin that was observed but extends the forgiveness to all of the brother's accumulated non-mortal sins. This restores the brother to a clean slate and returns his access to the Ask and Receive prayer.

SUMMARY OF THE ASK AND RECEIVE PRAYER

The Ask and Receive prayer is different from normal prayer because of the following two conditions.

- The person who prays must be born of God.
- The person who prays must be in a sinless state. Mortal sins are not relevant because anyone who is Born of God does not commit mortal sin, but non-mortal sins are of concern and must be cleared by confessing them to Jesus.

The Ask and Receive prayer can take two forms.

- Ask anything for anyone that is according to God's will.
- Ask specifically for the forgiveness of a brother's or sister's non-mortal sin(s).

This gift powerfully extends the means for those who are born of God to lovingly support their fellow brothers and sisters.

> *And this commandment we have from him, that he who loves God should love his brother also* (1 Jn 4:21).

Is John saying *not* to pray for those who are not yet born of God? No! John's focus here is only on the Ask and Receive prayer. Do not take it to mean anything else.

THIS GIFT EXPANDS THE OPPORTUNITIES FOR MORE LOVE AND LIFE!

Through this gift, God's plan is to encourage and support those who have mastered mortal sin to stay on the path of love by tending to "lesser" but nevertheless important sins which hinder God's children from seizing life to live it lovingly to the max in the here and now. Once again, we refer to Pope Benedict XVI on this.

> *"Eternal life" is life itself, real life, which can also be lived in the present age. . . This is the point: to seize "life" here and now, real life that can no longer be destroyed by anything or anyone.* [30]

CONCLUSION

GOD'S COMMANDMENT

John has presented the entire two-part commandment that is the core precept of Christianity to this day. It is the summation of what the Christians are to believe and use as a basis for their actions. It is the whole shebang condensed into two big points that cover everything.

> *And this is his commandment, that we should believe in the name of his Son Jesus Christ and love one another, just as he has commanded us* (1 Jn 3:23).

Every word of this commandment is of import. John testifies that he and the disciples received eternal life. They passed from death to life because they loved the brethren as God commanded. John as the beloved disciple and eyewitness is as qualified as anyone could be to explain the elements of the commandment.

- **What love is**—it is loving intention enacted as deeds that are according to the will of God. Carried to the farthest extent, such a deed would be to lay down one's life for another.
- **What love is not**—acts that are mortal sins such as murder, hate, and closing one's heart to a brother in need. Non-love can be both thoughts and actions.
- **Who Jesus is**—the Son of God who came in the flesh, who is both human and divine, not one or the other but both simultaneously.

---

[30] Joseph Ratzinger Pope Benedict XVI, *Jesus of Nazareth Part Two*, (San Francisco: Ignatius Press, 2011) 82.

ASK AND RECEIVE

John also announced a special and powerful form of prayer available to those who are born of God. God grants them the right to ask anything of God that is according to God's will and be assured he will grant it. This powerful prayer enables those who are born of God to help themselves and fellow children of God to live in the complete, loving capacity that God intends.

QUICK SUMMARY

In this chapter, John presents four pivotal elements of God's plan.

1. The new two-part Father's commandment: to believe in Jesus' name and to love one another
2. The need to love *not* by word and speech alone but in deed and in truth
3. The correct view of Jesus' identity as the Son of God and the Christ who is simultaneously divine and human
4. The Ask and Receive prayer that is available to those who are born of God

CHAPTER 8

The Reason to Love One Another and Believe
Spiral Text (1 John 4:7–5:13)

INTRODUCTION

THE SNAPSHOT

John is near the end of his letter; we will have only the climax to read after this chapter. What you will read in this chapter is a magnificent summary of the inexorable truth of the Christian message. All you need to do is read the headlines in the spiral text to obtain a preview of its logic. Here is a snapshot.

- The goal: love one another to be born of God.
- The approach: God sent his Son.
- The three roles of Jesus: the Son of God, the Christ, the human.
- How to carry the message forward—testimony and faith.
- Faith overcomes the world.

John does *not* provide a boring review of what he covered before. Far from it! He offers new nuggets of insight that direct you to the reasons you will want to do what he says. For example, this letter is known for its emphasis on love. John defines God as love; therefore, love is the only way to know God.

THE ANSWERS TO "WHY"

John will go one step further to answer the following all-important "why" questions.

- Why should people love one another?
- Why is God offering his gift?
- Why did he send his Son?
- Why love will reign over fear.

John will also answer the ultimate "why" question. He will explain why humankind can have success with love this time when they have failed so consistently before. He does this by explaining the four elements of the Father's commandment in detail. The commandment encapsulates everything we need to do to seize God's life now and forever.

John will conclude with God's plan to carry the message forward. His plan for witness and testimony is clearly the most successful the world has ever seen.

SPIRAL TEXT

ORIENTATION
Read the spiral text below to start your consideration of the text in this chapter.

1 JOHN 4:7–5:13

GOD'S PLAN
The Goal: Love One Another to Be Born of God

[4:7]Beloved let us love one another; for love is of God, and he who loves is born of God and knows God. [8]He who does not love does not know God; for God is love.

[4:11]Beloved, if God so loved us, we also ought to love one another. [12b]If we love one another, God abides in us and his love is perfected in us [13b]because he has given us of his own Spirit. [13a]By this we know that we abide in him and he in us.

The Approach: God Sent His Son

[4:12a]No man has ever seen God. [9a]In this, the love of God was made manifest among us that God sent his only Son into the world. [10]In this is love, not that we loved God but that he loved us and sent his Son to be the expiation for our sins, [9b]so that we might live through him.

Who Is Jesus?
Jesus Is the Son of God

[4:15]Whoever confesses that Jesus is the Son of God, God abides in him, and he in God. [16b]God is love, and he who abides in love abides in God. God abides in us [16a]so we know and believe the love God has for us. [19]We love, because he first loved us.

[4:17a]In this is love perfected with us. [18a]There is no fear in love, [18c]for fear has to do with punishment, and he who fears is not perfected in love, [18b]but perfect love casts out fear [17b]that we may have confidence for the day of judgment, because as he is so are we in this world.

Jesus the Son of God Is the Christ

[5:1]Everyone who believes that Jesus is the Christ is a child of God, and everyone who loves the parent loves the child. [2]By this we know that we love the children of God, when we love God and obey his commandments. [3]For this is the love of God, that we obey his commandments. And his commandments are not burdensome.

[4:20]If anyone says, "I love God," and hates his brother, he is a liar; for he who does not love his brother whom he has seen, cannot love God whom he has not seen. [21]And this commandment we have from him, that he who loves God should love his brother also.

Jesus Christ the Son of God Is the Fully Human Savior

[4:14]And we have seen and testify that the Father has sent his Son as the Savior of the world. [5:6]This is he who came by water and blood, not with the water only but with the water and the blood, Jesus Christ. [5:8a]There are three witnesses; [8c]and these three agree, [8c]the Spirit, the water, and the blood.

Testimony and Faith

Witness and Testimony

[5:7]And the Spirit is the witness, because the Spirit is the truth. [5:9]If we receive the testimony of men, the testimony of God is greater; for this is the testimony of God that he has borne witness to his Son. [10b]He who does not believe God has made him a liar, because he has not believed in the testimony that God has borne to his Son.

[5:10a]He who believes in the Son of God has the testimony in himself. [5:11]And this is the testimony that God gave us eternal life, and this life is in the Son. [5:12] He who has the Son has life; he who has not the Son of God has not life.

Our Faith Overcomes the World

[5:13]I write this to you who believe in the name of the Son of God, that you may know that you have eternal life. [5:4a]For whatever is born of God overcomes the world. [5:5]Who is it that overcomes the world but he who believes that Jesus is the Son of God? [5:4b]And this is the victory that overcomes the world, our faith.

COMMENTARY

THE GOAL: LOVE ONE ANOTHER TO BE BORN OF GOD

> **Spiral text:** [4:7]Beloved let us love one another; for love is of God, and he who loves is born of God and knows God. [8]He who does not love does not know God, for God is love.

THE SUMMATE PASSAGE

John opens with the passage that summarizes his entire letter.

> *Beloved, let us love one another; for love is of God, and he who loves is born of God and knows God* (1 Jn 4:7).

It summarizes the plan God puts before humankind.

- What to do—"let us love one another."
- Why do it—"for love is of God."
- The outcome—will be "born of God and know God."

This beautiful passage also introduces God to us—he is of love. Earlier, we said that John would explain the four components of the Father's commandment. This is where he takes up the love component.

GOD IS LOVE

Only here, in all Scripture, is God defined as love. John is saying love, not wrath, condemnation, or anything other than love is the basis for what God does. This places love at the heart of God's entire plan for humanity's salvation.

When believers commit to loving others and consistently enact their commitment, God fathers them. This opportunity for spiritual rebirth through love is the crux of God's new plan. Its benefits are breathtaking. However, to take advantage of them, humankind must literally shift their mental model of life itself. It is a paradigm shift to the most profound degree.

WHAT IS THE PARADIGM SHIFT?

Since the time of Adam and Eve life ended in permanent death; however Jesus' resurrection changed that. He brought eternal life, which changed the paradigm. The paradigm shift is for people to realize that life no longer has to end; eternal life in God's loving presence is available again.

> ". . . *lest he put forth his hand and take also of the tree of life, and eat, and live forever*"—*therefore the LORD God sent him forth from the garden of Eden . . .* (Gen 3:22–23).

God did not intend for eternal death to be the state of man.

> *For God created man for incorruption, and made him in the image of his own <u>eternity</u>, but through the devil's envy death entered the world, and those who belong to his party experience it* (Wisdom 2:23–24).

God's restoration of eternal life represents a 180° turning point in humankind's relationship with him and each other. People now have the opportunity to choose between:

- Changing their ways by actively loving one another to *know* and live with a loving God eternally, or
- Remain the same by continuing to pursue non-loving, self-oriented behavior that leads to life that terminates in permanent death.

PERFECTED LOVE

Spiral text: [4:11]Beloved, if God so loved us, we also ought to love one another. [12b]If we love one another, God abides in us and his love is perfected in us [13b]because he has given us of his own Spirit. [13a]By this we know that we abide in him and he in us.

THEY OUGHT TO LOVE

John tells his audience they ought to love one another, plain and simple. When they do, they are in effect signing up to receive life with God. This is how they tell God that they, of their freewill, choose him. Look at what it will bring.

1. A life lived in the presence of God's love now and forever versus the alternative of a life lived without *knowing* God ending in permanent death (1 Jn 5:18)
2. A life untouched by the world's evil (1 Jn 5:18)
3. A life free of mortal sin (1 Jn 3:9)
4. A loving life with God that they will not lose (1 Jn 5:18)

HOW PERFECTED LOVE IS ACTIVATED

John uses the term, *perfected love* to describe what happens to the love between God and those who are born of him. To become perfected means that something becomes more perfect than it was, but this could not be God's love, for it is already perfect. So what does John mean when he says God's love is perfected?

When believers love one another so completely they become born of God, it means that God's love abides in them through the Holy Spirit. By this, they know God abides in them and they in him. From that point forward, only love defines a believer's relationship with God, which is when love is perfected (completed) in the believer.

Will humankind change their ways toward love? Evil still reigns in the world, but there is reason to hope.

THE APPROACH: GOD SENT HIS SON

Spiral text: ⁴:¹²ᵃNo man has ever seen God. ⁹ᵃIn this, the love of God was made manifest among us that God sent his only Son into the world. ¹⁰In this is love, not that we loved God but that he loved us and sent his Son to be the expiation for our sins, ⁹ᵇso that we might live through him.

WHY WILL THINGS BE DIFFERENT THIS TIME?

God has commanded his children to love one another from the beginning.

> *You shall not take vengeance or bear any grudge against the sons of your own people, but you shall love your neighbor as yourself: I am the LORD* (Lev 19:18).

They never succeeded. Is there anything that will enable them to be different this time? The answer is a resounding yes!

God sent his only Son to the world so people could have a living demonstration of God's love to see, hear, and believe that God was actually restoring access to eternal life. No one had ever seen God before.

> *"And the Father who sent me . . . His voice you have never heard, his form you have never seen . . ."* (Jn 5:37b).

The adage "seeing is believing" was as operational in John's day as it is today. Jesus, who was in plain sight fully visible for everyone to see, was to be the voice of the Father.

> . . . *"What I say, therefore, I say as the Father has bidden me"* (Jn 12:50).

WHAT WILL THE SON DO?

If we presume that an all-powerful God could have simply restored eternal life, but instead chose to send his Son, what was the Son sent to do? For starters, he is the expiation for sin. Expiation nullifies the consequences of past sins; it forgives a person's accumulation of sins to provide a fresh start.

God intended the Son's expiation to be for everyone, but to receive it, people must accept God's gift of his Son, which entails two things.

- Believing Jesus is God's Son
- Being willing to do the one thing Jesus said to do—love one another

At this point, acceptance of God's gift does not require actually doing the loving deeds that John talked about earlier; it is only to take the first step—to be willing to make the commitment to love. Since seeing is believing, let us look at the meaning of expiation in light of Jesus' visible death and resurrection.

HOW EXPIATION WORKS

Expiation is not a pagan-like sacrifice made as appeasement for sin. God is love; he is not a wrathful God who requires retribution. Expiation points to Jesus' death and resurrection as the confirmation of God's love of humankind and his granting eternal life through his Son. Jesus' resurrection enabled people to do the following:

- Realize he is the Son of God
- Fathom that eternal life is possible

Death did not defeat Jesus; instead, he visibly demonstrated eternal life. By this, how can people *not* accept the fact that God sent his Son? When they believe Jesus is the Son of God, they will be released from the heavy load of their past sins to make eternal life a possibility.

> *"I am the light of the world; he who follows me will not walk in darkness, but will have the light of life"* (Jn 8:12).

According to scholar Raymond Brown, Jesus' actions take on the sense of cleansing a believer's impurity, which has the effect of forgiveness.[31] This gives them a clean slate to begin converting their life of sin into a life of love.

By Jesus' resurrection, which is the greatest demonstration of God's love in the history of the world, the Son made belief in God's love possible. Many prophets had come before, but Jesus' resurrection confirmed that the true Son of God was on earth, died, rose again, and lives on. This is the heart of God's new plan. The Son made it all visible.

---

[31] Raymond E. Brown, Translation with Introduction, Notes, and Commentary, *The Anchor Bible: The Epistles of John* (New York: Doubleday, 1982) 219–221.

JESUS IS THE SON OF GOD

Spiral text: [4:15]Whoever confesses that Jesus is the Son of God, God abides in him, and he in God. [16b]God is love, and he who abides in love abides in God. God abides in us [16a]so we know and believe the love God has for us. [19]We love, because he first loved us.

[4:17a]In this is love perfected with us. [18a]There is no fear in love, [18c]for fear has to do with punishment, and he who fears is not perfected in love, [18b]but perfect love casts out fear [17bc]that we may have confidence for the day of judgment because as he is so are we in this world.

WHY CONFESS THE SON OF GOD?

This is where John explains the first of the three aspects of Jesus' name. Jesus is the Son of God, whom God sent to grant eternal life. Jesus the Son determines when a believer is ready to receive eternal life and serves as the believer's Advocate with the Father to support his journey to a love-based life.

> *"And I know that his commandment is eternal life . . . "* (Jn 12:50).

A person who does *not* believe Jesus is God's only Son incarnate would *not* have reason to believe Jesus could offer eternal life. He or she would *not* believe Jesus had seen God or heard God express his wishes. Therefore, Jesus would *not* be any more credible than any other person who offers wise words. In fact, Jesus's own statement about his role would make *not* make sense.

> . . . *"I am the way, and the truth, and the life; no one comes to the Father, but by me"* (Jn 14:6).

Jesus is unlike any prophet or anointed one who has gone before. Jesus is *not* simply the Christ; he is the Son of God! Those who do not confess Jesus as God's Son cannot receive God's gift of life because it is only available through his Son.

WHAT DOES CONFESS MEAN?

To confess is to declare agreement with something.[32] To confess Jesus as the Son of God is to agree with God about the following:

- Jesus is the Son of God—he is God's love made manifest.
- Jesus is truthful when he says eternal life is available.
- Jesus is correct when he says a person must abide in love to receive eternal life.

When people reach their moment to confess the Son, it means they have come to understand and believe how much God loves them. They realize that by his restoration of eternal life, God does indeed love them first and because of this, their response is to love God in return. A confession that Jesus is the Son of God indicates a person is willing to make the turn toward love. If these people stay on the love track, God will abide in them.

LOVE IS PERFECTED WITH US

Earlier, we noted God gives a believer his Spirit when he or she sufficiently loves one another. Through the Spirit, such believers know God abides in them and they in him, which indicates God's love is perfected in them. Here, John says God's love is perfected <u>with us</u>. How is this different?

Love perfected with us is the absence of fear within those who are born of God. They can have confidence in anticipation of the Day of Judgment because with no mortal sins, they have no punishable offenses to be judged.

> *. . . he who was born of God keeps him, and the evil one does not touch him* (1 Jn 5:18).

Therefore, their anticipation about their entire future can be free and fearless because God's Spirit is with them to protect and guide them from the evil of the world.

---

[32] http://classic.net.bible.org/strong.php?id=3670.

AS HE IS SO ARE WE

Those born of God share three important aspects with Jesus.

- They are in mutual and eternal union with God as Jesus is.[33] In his Farewell Prayer, Jesus confirms the possibility for this to occur.

  "... that they may all be one; even as thou Father, art in me, and I in thee, that also may be in us..." (Jn 17:21).

- They have complete love for God as Jesus does.

  "... but I do as the Father has commanded me, so that the world may know that I love the Father ... " (Jn 14:31).

- Jesus is God's only Son. Those who are born of God are fathered by God so they are God's children somewhat like Jesus;[34] however, Jesus is the *only* begotten (capital S) Son.

Now that we have looked at Jesus as God's Son who grants eternal life on an individual basis, let us look at the role of Jesus as the Christ, which is different.

JESUS THE SON OF GOD IS THE CHRIST

Spiral text: [5:1]everyone who believes that Jesus is the Christ is a child of God, and everyone who loves the parent loves the child. [5:2]By this, we know that we love the children of God, when we love God and obey his commandments. [5:3]For this is the love of God, that we obey his commandments. And his commandments are not burdensome. [4:20]If anyone says, "I love God," and hates his brother, he is a liar; for he who does not love his brother whom he has seen, cannot love God whom he has not

---

[33] Raymond E. Brown, Translation with Introduction, Notes, and Commentary, *The Anchor Bible: The Epistles of John* (New York: Doubleday, 1982) 529.

[34] Ibid.

not seen. [21]And this commandment we have from him, that he who loves God should love his brother also.

JESUS IS THE CHRIST

John describes Jesus the Christ as the Jesus who is concerned with the world's salvation and the creation of God's worldwide family. This family is made up of children of God. John begins by defining three things: who is in God's family, how to become a member of the family, and how to love family members. He does this by linking all three to the keeping of the Father's commandments.

- A person enters into God's family as a child of God by obeying God's commandments.
- A person loves God by keeping the commandments.
- A person loves God's children by keeping his commandments and loving God.

It may appear that John is going over familiar ground here, but he has actually revealed two new and significant points.

- How to love God
- How to love God's children

The answer is the same in both cases: obey God's commandments. Next, John will expand what it means to keep the commandment to love one another.

EXPANDED LOVE

John states anyone who cannot love <u>every</u> brother/sister is *not* a child of God. If they claim to be, they are liars. The reason is simple. One cannot love and hate God at the same time. These brothers/sisters have received God's seed; they abide in God and God in them. Therefore, to hate a brother/sister is to hate a part of God.

Such love is not burdensome. Here's the reason. These brothers/sisters have made the commitment to love, which they enact as their ongoing lifestyle. All of them, whether they are strangers or not, are loving people, so how hard would it be to love them?

JESUS CHRIST THE SON OF GOD IS
THE FULLY HUMAN SAVIOR

Spiral text: [4:14]And we have seen and testify that the Father has sent his Son as the Savior of the world. [5:6]This is he who came by water and blood, not with the water only but with the water and the blood, Jesus Christ. [8a]There are three witnesses; [8c]and these three agree, [8b]the Spirit, the water, and the blood.

BLOOD, WATER, AND SPIRIT

John will tell us about Jesus' humanity and his mission on earth through the use of three terms: *blood*, *water*, and *spirit*. We are going to connect John's use of *water*, *blood*, and *Spirit* to pivotal passages in his Gospel to convey the core components of God's plan.

1. They indicate Jesus God's Son is fully human (water and blood).
2. They describe the two gifts he brings (the water and the blood).
   o Forgive sin
   o Grant eternal life
3. They indicate when the gifts become available (the Spirit, the water, and the blood).

BY *WATER* AND *BLOOD* INDICATE JESUS' HUMANITY

In his Gospel, John indicates Jesus came in the flesh and was made manifest by telling us that directly.

And the Word became flesh and dwelt among us . . . (Jn 1:14).

He also uses the terms *water* and *blood* as indicators of Jesus' humanity. For example, when Jesus discussed being born anew in Spirit with Nicodemus, he used *water* as an analogy for human birth.

> "... unless one is born of <u>water</u> and the Spirit, he cannot enter the kingdom of God" (Jn 3:5).

John used *blood* as an analogy for human birth in the prologue to his Gospel.

> ... who were born <u>not</u> of <u>blood</u>, nor of the will of the flesh ... but of God (Jn 1:13).

Jesus' humanity enables people to believe God's plan is to restore eternal life because God's Son Jesus, the human, died a physical death yet rose from it.

> If Christ has not been raised, then our preaching is in vain and your faith is in vain (1Cor 15:13–14).

WITH <u>THE WATER</u> AND <u>THE BLOOD</u> AS JESUS' INSTRUMENTS

When John prefaces *water* and *blood* with the Greek word *en*,[35] which in the RSV translation is the word *the*—<u>the</u> water and <u>the</u> blood, he is saying something different from the prior passage. There, John treated *water* and *blood* as one component. It was as though they went together like a hand in a glove. Here, he separates them to indicate Jesus' two purposes. He came to be the expiation for sins and to grant eternal life.

> To be the expiation for our sins, so that we might live through him (1 Jn 4:9a–10–9b spiral text).

Jesus performs his two purposes as the Son of God with <u>the</u> water and <u>the</u> blood. These are what make it possible for humanity to succeed at love this time around.

1. The blood from Jesus' body was the expiation for sin.

> ... and the blood of Jesus his Son cleanses us from all sin (1 Jn 1:7b).

---

[35] Raymond E. Brown, S.S., *The Anchor Bible; v. 30*, "The Epistles of John" (New York: Doubleday, 1982) 573–575.

2. The living water from the Son of God will well up to provide access to eternal life.

> *". . . but whoever drinks of the water that I shall give him will never thirst; the water . . . will become in him a spring of water welling up to eternal life"* (Jn 4:13–14).

When did these two gifts become available?

WHEN THE GIFTS BECAME AVAILABLE

Both the expiation of sin and the granting of eternal life became available upon Jesus' glorification—his death and resurrection. How is John telling us this? Let us look at the only time other than the passage we are considering, that John mentions *spirit, water,* and *blood* together.

When Jesus was on the cross, he declared it finished and gave up his *Spirit.* This is when one of the soldiers pierced his side and Jesus' *blood* and *water* came out. This tells us the Spirit, blood, and water were there. They witnessed what happened.

> *. . . he said, "It is finished"; and he bowed his head and gave up his <u>spirit</u>'. . . one of the soldiers pierced his side with a spear, and at once there came out <u>blood and water</u>* (Jn 19:30; 34).

In his Gospel, John told us the significance of the "hour" of Jesus' glorification. First, he identified when it occurred. Then he clearly stated that only upon this hour could Jesus grant the Holy Spirit, which brings eternal life.

> *When Jesus had spoken these words, he lifted up his eyes to heaven and said, 'Father, the hour has come glorify thy Son that the Son may glorify thee* (Jn 17:1).

> *Now this he said about the Spirit, which those who believed in him were to receive; for as yet the Spirit had not been given, because Jesus was not yet glorified* (Jn 7:39).

The transition of Jesus' glorification is the decisive point of the Christian faith. The water, blood, and Spirit were there to witness it, and John says they agree. To what do they all agree?

THE THREE WITNESSES AGREE

The three witnesses agree to Jesus' humanity. The water and blood were present from the time of his birth, and the Spirit arrived at the beginning of his ministry. John the Baptist bore witness to this.

> *And John bore witness, "I saw the Spirit descend as a dove from heaven, and it remained on him"* (Jn 1:32).

All three witnesses left Jesus at the time of his physical death, so the only thing they can testify in unison to is the fact Jesus came in the flesh. They were all with him until the end of his physical life. Jesus' physical blood and water could *not* live past his physical death, but God's Spirit does. It plays the pivotal role in the next step of God's plan, which deals with testimony.

RECAP OF WHAT IT MEANS TO BELIEVE IN JESUS' NAME

The first part of the Father's commandment is to believe in the name of his Son Jesus Christ (1 Jn 3:23). John has told us what belief in his name means by dealing with each of the three parts of his name separately. Jesus is simultaneously:

1. The Son of God, who provides eternal life on an individual-by-individual basis.
2. The Christ, who came to save the world by the creation of a family composed of God's children.
3. The human, who proved that eternal life with God is available by his death and resurrection.

To believe in Jesus' name is to be in agreement with all three aspects.

JESUS THE HUMAN FULFILLED HIS MISSION; WHAT IS NEXT?

Jesus is the heart and soul of humankind's ability to make the 180° turn toward love. He is God's Son, the Christ who came in the flesh to open the gate to eternal life and support a person's journey there. God commanded eternal life to Jesus and he obeyed.

"And I know that his commandment is eternal life. What I say,
therefore, I say as the Father has bidden me" (Jn 12:50).

Jesus is the only human in the history of the world who died to rise again. By this, he propelled the existence of eternal life onto the world's stage. No one could have believed it was possible before. His compelling demonstration of eternal life is the reason he says that no one comes to the Father but by me. Yet, we must ask, will people buy it? Everything hinges on people believing that God restored eternal life through his Son. If people do not believe it, they will not be able to receive it.

The next phase of God's plan addresses this crucial issue. It provides for the systematic communication about eternal life through witness and testimony, which John will take up next.

WITNESS AND TESTIMONY

Spiral text: 5:7And the Spirit is the witness because the Spirit is the truth. 5:9If we receive the testimony of men, the testimony of God is greater; for this is the testimony of God that he has borne witness to his Son. 11He, who does not believe God, has made him (God) a liar, because he has not believed in the testimony that God has borne to his Son.

5:10He who believes in the Son of God has the testimony in himself. 11And this is the testimony that God gave us eternal life, and this life is in the Son. 12He who has the Son has life; he who has not the Son of God has not life.

THE PURPOSE OF GOD'S WITNESS AND TESTIMONY PLAN

The purpose of God's witness and testimony plan is for humankind to believe two things.

- Jesus is the Son of God.
- Jesus brings eternal life to humanity.

Belief in Jesus is the fulcrum that leads to the loving behavior that secures eternal life. When it is received, believers have the Spirit within them, which is what the scriptural text refers to when it says *the testimony of God is greater*. However, to reach this point, the "lesser" testimony of men is absolutely necessary.

MAN'S TESTIMONY IS THE LINCHPIN

This may be a surprise, but man's testimony is the linchpin of the plan. Here's the reason. After Jesus' death and his brief time on earth afterward, the only way people can be introduced to Jesus is through another human. It is human testimony that lights and kindles the spark so it can grow into the mighty flame of faith that leads to the receipt of Spirit.

Initial exposure to Jesus may come from a family member, a pastor or priest, a trusted friend, or even a total stranger. It has to start from someone—a human. Jesus' handoff to human testimony began when he *sent* his disciples after he gave them the Holy Spirit.

They proclaimed and taught the message of eternal life. Their direct writings have survived to reach us through Scripture. John is one of those eyewitnesses. When you read this letter, you are reading John's direct witness of Jesus, the Son of God, who died and rose again. You are receiving the power, passion, and conviction of what John saw, heard, and experienced. No matter how much credibility anyone who lives today has, that person cannot communicate God's truth as John conveys it.

The table below shows the progression from faith to ultimate knowing, with faith in men's/women's testimony being pivotal to reaching that goal.

TABLE 8-1. PROGRESSION FROM FAITH TO KNOWING

Initiation		Implementation	Completion
God's testimony (God)	God's testimony (Jesus)	Men and women's testimony	God's testimony (Spirit)
God testifies to John the Baptist	The glorified Jesus testifies to the disciples; they receive the Spirit	Men/women testify to the world	People who are are born of God receive the Spirit's testimony
John the Baptist introduces Jesus	The disciples tell others	Some people develop faith in Jesus	They know

GOD BORE WITNESS TO HIS SON

God launched his witness and testimony plan as the first to testify to his Son. He bore witness to John the Baptist who bore witness to Israel that Jesus is the Son of God.

> *"And I have seen and bore witness that this is the Son of God"* (Jn 1:34).

John the Baptist knew Jesus was God's Son because God told him the person on whom he sees the Spirit descend and remain is his Son.

> *". . . but he who sent me to baptize with water said to me, 'He on whom you see the Spirit descend and remain, this is he who baptizes with the Holy Spirit'"* (Jn 1:33).

A valid witness must have personally heard, seen, or experienced that to which he or she testifies, which is what God set in motion with John the

Baptist. After John the Baptist testified to the Jews, he told two of his disciples that Jesus was the Lamb of God, which led to their following Jesus.

> *The next day . . . he looked at Jesus as he walked, and said, "Behold the Lamb of God!" The two disciples heard him say this, and they followed Jesus* (Jn 1:35–37).

JESUS BEARS WITNESS AND SENDS HIS DISCIPLES

The glorified Jesus launched the next phase of the communications chain when he came to the disciples on the third day and gave them the Spirit. This is also when he commissioned them to serve as his witnesses to the truth.

> *. . . he showed them his hands and his side. Then the disciples were glad when they saw the Lord . . . "As the Father has sent me, even so I send you" . . . he breathed on them, and said to them, "Receive the Holy Spirit"* (Jn 20:20–22).

THE SPIRIT BEARS WITNESS

Jesus grants God's Spirit to those who keep the Father's commandments. The coming of the Spirit of Truth to abide within a person brings the testimony of God within the person. Instead of depending on man's testimony, they now know for themselves.

> *. . . the anointing which you received from him abides in you, and you have no need that any one should teach you; as his anointing teaches you about everything, and is true . . .* (1 Jn 2:27).

This anointing is a major shift in the way things worked before. In the past, only very holy men such as Moses or Elijah have had the Spirit within them; now it is available to everyone who is born of God. Next let us look at how John says this will occur.

OUR FAITH OVERCOMES THE WORLD

Spiral text: [5:13]I write this to you who believe in the name of the Son of God, that you may know that you have eternal life. [5:4a]For whatever is born of God overcomes the world. [5:5]Who is it that overcomes the world but he who believes that Jesus is the Son of God? [4b]And this is the victory that overcomes the world, our faith.

FAITH IN MAN'S TESTIMONY

John says the way to receive the Holy Spirit is to overcome the world, and can only be accomplished through faith. However, let us point out, people do not lack for faith! The issue is where they choose to place their faith. The victory that John speaks of comes from having faith in Jesus God's Son instead of worldly people or things. The issue of faith comes down to choice. John urges his readers to choose to put their faith in God's Son. This is the very reason he writes this letter!

WHERE FAITH TAKES YOU

Faith is trust without proof. It is what drives behavior when there is no guarantee of the outcome. Who can guarantee what God will do? No one can; however, when people trust humans such as the writers of Scripture, pastors, priests, teachers, and others who communicate about Jesus, enough to believe in Jesus the Son and keep his commandment to love one another, they have the opportunity to come to know God in a way that goes beyond faith.

The witness of the Spirit within infinitely surpasses faith! By receipt of the Holy Spirit, people can *know* God's love from within themselves on a moment-by-moment basis for eternity.

CONCLUSION

GOD'S PLAN FOR A BELIEVER IN A NUTSHELL

The plan God puts before humankind is the following:

- What to do—Love one another.
- Why do it—God loves us.
- The outcome—to be able to seize life with God now and forever.

God sent his Son to implement this plan. His incarnation is the fundamental reason humans can succeed at love this time. Seeing is believing and Jesus demonstrates the power of God's love by his visible defeat of death. No one before Jesus could do this, but he did, and it is the basis for a worldwide paradigm shift in one's conception of life. It no longer must end in death; it can be eternal.

To confess Jesus is to agree that Jesus is God's Son incarnate who came to forgive sin and offer eternal life. It is also belief in him as the Christ who came to build a worldwide family of the new children of God who of their freewill choose God through their love. This chapter answered how a person should love God and the children of this family. There is only one way—keep God's two-fold commandment to believe in Jesus and love one another.

IMPLEMENTATION OF GOD'S PLAN

Having covered the New Covenant, John concludes Part II with God's plan for implementation. Think of it! What God started over 2,000 years ago through his Son and twelve disciples has grown to billions! It was launched with God's testimony to just one man, John the Baptist, which led to Jesus testifying to his disciples, who testified to others through their spoken and written word. You are reading the testimony of one of these eyewitness disciples in this letter!

Believe and Love
Spiral Text (1:8–2:28; 3:11–5:17)

THE ORGANIZATION OF PART II

In Part I, John announced God's New Covenant with humankind and its magnificent benefits. God's plan is to restore eternal life. This time, he intends it for the entire world and is sending his Son to implement it. Jesus is going to make it possible for humanity to succeed this time.

Part II of this letter reveals in detail, exactly what humankind will need to do to receive life with God again. In a nutshell, it is to keep the Father's commandments, which is to believe in God's Son and to love one another. John declares that these requirements are not burdensome.

John organizes the second part of the letter in four parts, as he did Part I. The table below is a look back and a look forward of the entire letter. It depicts the four organizational elements that John uses in both, Part I and Part II. John concludes the letter with the simple statement of choice that comes next, in Part III.

TABLE 8-2. OVERVIEW OF 1 JOHN

#	ORGANIZING ELEMENT	PART I: ETERNAL LIFE Chapter 3	PART II: KEEP HIS COMMANDMENTS Chapters 4-8
1.	The setting	Jesus tells the disciples to proclaim the restoration of eternal life with God	God sends Jesus to assist humanity so they can have eternal fellowship with God this time
2.	The message	Walk in the light as God is light	Love one another and believe in Jesus' name to walk in the light
3.	The two sides of the covenant	God will restore eternal life	Humankind needs to keep the Father's commandment, which is to believe in Jesus' name and to love one another
4.	John's advice	Keep away from idols	Have faith in man's testimony about Jesus
PART III: CHAPTER 9			
Choose to purify or sin			

GOD'S PLAN

The crux of God's plan is the restoration of love as the basis for the way the world works. God sent his Son to save the world and restore the opportunity for eternal life, who through his love of the Father, chose to do as the Father bid him. In Part II, John told his audience to do the same.

> *Beloved, let us love one another;, for love is of God, and he who loves is born of God and knows God.* (1 Jn 4:7).

The components of God's plan that come in the form of the New Covenant are the heart of the compelling Christian message that has been going strong for 2,000 years. So what is next? In Part III, John will ask his audience to choose. Will it be God or the world? Their freewill gives them the right to decide.

"Beloved, we are God's children now. . . we know that when he appears we shall be like him, for we shall see him as he is" (1 Jn 3:2).

3

The Choice is Yours

CHAPTER 9

The Choice: Purify or Sin

Spiral Text (2:29–3:10)

INTRODUCTION

This first letter's steady climb reaches its crescendo in this chapter. John highlights the following points to take you to the last and most important message of the entire letter.

- Aim to do right to become born of God; this is the target.
- The Father's gift is the opportunity to become children of God.
- Sin is the challenge. Jesus appeared to take away sins.
- God's children cannot sin because God's nature abides in them.

- Do not let anyone deceive you. The choice is yours to do right and purify yourself or sin and continue as a child of the devil.

John hones in on what it takes to be born of God—"do what is right," which is *to not* sin. Those who sin are children of the devil, but John's message is that everyone can choose a different father now! Humankind can choose to follow God or the devil. This chapter asks which it will be.

The stakes are a matter of life or death as the opening passage of the *Didache*, an early 2nd century teaching document also attests. This document only re-discovered in 1873, describes the earliest stages of the practices of the church.[36] It opens with the very choice that John lays out for his audience in this chapter.

> *There are two ways, one of life and one of death! and there is a great difference between the two ways* (1:1).

This opening which parallels John's premise, indicates that John's writings had been embraced more widely than by those of his community. *The Didache* known as the *Doctrine by the Apostles* was a widely accepted and popular treatise[37] in the early Church.

SPIRAL TEXT

ORIENTATION

Read the spiral text below to start your consideration of the text in this chapter.

1 JOHN 2:29–3:10

The Goal Is to Be Born of God

[2:29]If you know that he is righteous, you may be sure that everyone who does right is born of him. [10b]Whoever does not do right is not of God, nor he who does not love his brother.

To Become Children of God

[3:1a]See what love the Father has given us that we should be called children of God; and so we are. [3:2]Beloved, we are God's children now; it does "not yet" appear what we shall, but we know that when he appears we shall be like him, for we shall see him as he is.

---

[36] http://www.earlychristianwritings.com/info/didache.html

[37] http://www.earlychristianwritings.com/tixeront/section1-1.html#didache

Sin Is the Worldly Challenge

[3:1b]The reason why the world does not know us is that it did not know him. [5]You know that he appeared to take away sins, in him there is no sin. [6]No one who abides in him sins; no one who sins has either seen him or known him. [8]He who commits sin is of the devil; for the devil has sinned from the beginning. The reason the Son of God appeared was to destroy the works of the devil.

Receive God's Seed

[3:9a]No one born of God commits sin, [9c]and he cannot sin because he is born of God; [9b]for God's nature abides in him.

The Choice: Purify or Sin

[10a]By this it may be seen who the children of God are and who are the children of the devil. [7]Little children, let no one deceive you. He who does right is righteous, as he is righteous. [3]And everyone who thus hopes in him purifies himself as he is pure. [4]Everyone who commits sin is guilty of lawlessness; sin is lawlessness.

COMMENTARY

THE GOAL IS TO BE BORN OF GOD

Spiral text: [2:29]If you know that he is righteous you may be sure that everyone who does right is born of him. [3:10b]Whoever does not do right is not of God, nor he who does not love his brother.

ETERNAL LIFE—TO BE BORN OF GOD

John begins this climatic conclusion the same way he began this letter—with the overarching theme of eternal life. This will be John's last opportunity to drive home the target of being born of God. He will do it simply and compellingly by landing on the fundamental choice each person has—to do right or to sin.

WHY DOES JOHN SAY JESUS IS RIGHTEOUS?

To *not* do right (to sin) defines a person as *not* of God. To do right is to want to do the will of God, but *not* out of obedience for obedience sake. True righteousness comes from love.

John uses the word *righteous* in only one other place outside of this chapter where he announced Jesus as the sinner's Advocate. This is John's way of saying a sinner does *not* have to deal with his or her sin alone. God sent Jesus to help by forgiving sin.

> *. . . But if any one does sin, we have an advocate with the Father, Jesus Christ the righteous* (1 Jn 2:1).

Next, John will paint the glorious picture of what God's loving gift of his Son will bring to those who choose him. First however, John brings our attention to his experience as a disciple to back up what he is about to say.

TO BECOME CHILDREN OF GOD

Spiral text: ³:¹ªSee what love the Father has given us that we should be called children of God; and so we are. ³:²Beloved, we are God's children now; it does "not yet" appear what we shall, but we know that when he appears we shall be like him, for we shall see him as he is.

JOHN THE EYEWITNESS ANNOUNCES WHAT GOD'S CHILDREN WILL RECEIVE

As he has done before, John calls on his authority as an eyewitness of the resurrected Jesus to authenticate what he says.

> *. . . and we saw it, and testify to it, and proclaim to you the eternal life which was with the Father and was made manifest to us* (1 Jn 1:2).

John provides an amazing picture of what will happen when Jesus appears again. Having already seen Jesus "as he is" in his glorified state, John knows that when God's children see Jesus as he is, they will be like him—pure and sinless. Their love of the Father and the Father's love for his children have made this possible.

> *"And when I go and prepare a place for you, I will come again and will take you to myself, that where I am you may be also"* (Jn 14:3).

SIN IS THE WORLDLY CHALLENGE

> **Spiral text**: [3:1b]The reason why the world does not know us is that it did not know him [5]You know that he appeared to take away sins, in him there is no sin. [6]No one who abides in him sins; no one who sins has either seen him or known him. [8]He who commits sin is of the devil, for the devil has sinned from the beginning. The reason the Son of God appeared was to destroy the works of the devil.

CHILDREN OF THE DEVIL

Those who overcome the world are those who believe Jesus is the Son of God and by this, receive his forgiveness of sin and are cleansed. By contrast, those who do not *believe,* do sin. They are children of a different parent—the devil. They do *not* do what is right.

> *We know that we are of God, and the whole world is in the power of the evil one* (1 Jn 5:19).

The reason Jesus came in the first place is to take away sin, and thereby, destroy the works of the devil.

> . . . *"Behold, the Lamb of God, who takes away the sin of the world!"* (Jn 1:29).

This is the point! Those who are children of God do what is right. They will have the opportunity to be like Jesus in his glorified state.

RECEIVE GOD'S SEED

Spiral text: [3:9a]No one born of God commits sin, [9c]and he cannot sin because he is born of God; [9b]for God's nature abides in him.

WHAT IS JOHN SAYING?

These two parallel statements about sin are John's efficient and elegant way to synthesize the before and after phases of eternal life.

1. Does not commit sin is what the person who wishes to become born of God does when he or she keeps God's commandments.
2. Cannot sin is what happens after one is born of God. God protects his children from the evil one and therefore, from sin.

> *... but he who was born of God keeps him, and the evil one does not touch him* (1 Jn 5:18).

The first statement—*does not commit sin*, is the before phase. It is how believers indicate they want to live in God's loving presence. They opt in by choosing of their freewill to keep God's commandments to live a non-sinning lifestyle. This leads to the after phase when they are born of God.

> *All who keep his commandments abide in him, and he in them* (1 Jn 3:24).

THE TRANSFORMATION

Being born of God is the moment a person crosses over from being a sinner (mortal sin) to someone who has developed a lifestyle of not sinning, and who is ready to receive the ongoing state of being whereby he or she cannot sin mortally. This occurs when God infuses his loving nature through the Holy Spirit to stay in the person.

THE CHOICE: PURIFY OR SIN

> **Spiral text:** [3:10a]By this it may be seen who the children of God are and who are the children of the devil. [3:7]Little children, let no one deceive you. He who does right is righteous, as he is righteous. [3:3]And everyone who thus hopes in him purifies himself, as he is pure. [3:4]Everyone who commits sin is guilty of lawlessness; sin is lawlessness.

THE CHOICE

John wraps up this letter at the point of critical choice. In prior passages, John has told his audience the antichrists are out there, and just as the serpent deceived Adam and Eve, his progeny will attempt to do the same. John tells his audience how to discern who they are. They are lawbreakers who have contempt for God's commands and make *no* attempt to purify.

THE FINAL WORD

People have the opportunity to choose their fate. They have freewill. The time to turn to love is now, for they have no other life. The option is theirs—to live forever with a loving God or live in contempt of God's command to love and die a permanent death. Which will it be, God or the devil?

A child of sin   The Devil ⟺ God   A child of love

CONCLUSION

GOD'S PLAN COMES DOWN TO OUR FREEWILL

John's final message is that, ultimately, eternal life lies in our hands. We are at choice.

- Do we listen to the deceivers? John tells us how to discern who they are.
- Do we love a brother? John says this is how you love God.
- Do we confess our sin to Jesus? John tells us Jesus is our Advocate and will forgive our sins. His mission is to destroy the devil.

- Do we show contempt for the law as Adam and Eve did or do we choose God's will because we love God? John tells is to take the righteous path.

John then depicts the magnificent outcome of making the loving choice.

We shall see Jesus as he is and shall be like him!

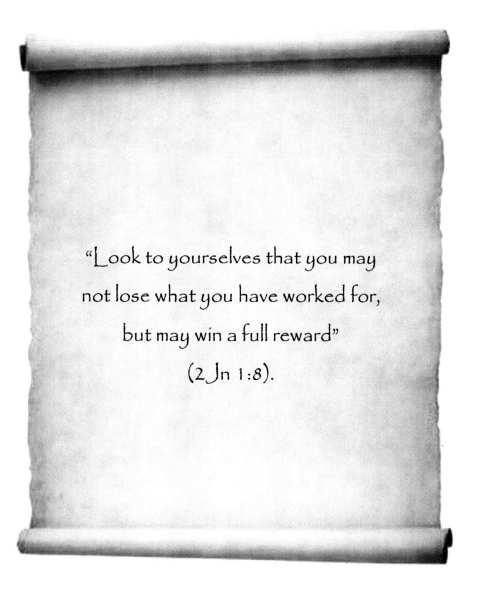

"Look to yourselves that you may not lose what you have worked for, but may win a full reward" (2 Jn 1:8).

Life Examples in

2 & 3 John

PART IV

Life Examples in 2 & 3 John

INTRODUCTION

PURPOSE

John's first letter thoroughly explained the principles of eternal life. However, what can look so clear on paper can become fuzzy and distorted when it comes to application. The two letters we are about to explore are real-life examples of issues that arise in the application of the two precepts of the Father's commandment.

The issues John touches on are so relevant you could find them on today's online discussion boards. Here are a few.

- How to be "inclusive" when people who intend to dissuade the congregation from believing in Jesus want to give talks in the church.
- Is the Christian obligation to welcome all brothers/sisters in Christ?
- What to do when doing the loving deed feels non-loving?
- How church leaders can figure out how to protect and guide their flock in face of conflict within.

John's approach to finding the right answer is like bedrock—it is always to seek the truth, no matter what issue is at hand. In these two letters, he will direct us to the two foundational elements of God's plan that make the truth discernible.

THE TWO FOUNDATIONAL ELEMENTS

At their heart, these letters focus on the two core precepts of the Father's commandment to believe and love. John will use situations at two outlying churches to take up two types of mortal sin.

1. In 2 John, he deals with a mortal sin related to whether Jesus the Son is the Christ incarnate.
2. In 3 John he deals with a mortal sin related to the love of a brother/sister in Christ.

RELEVANCY OF THE LETTERS FOR TODAY

The 21st century has not brought new answers to these topics; it has only made their application more complex. In today's information laden world, you can find differing opinions of every nuanced variation of these issues on web sites, blogs, and countless talk shows, 24/7. However, is everyone's point of view necessary to make a wise decision?

When you read these letters, see for yourself whether John's authority as the beloved disciple, who was with Jesus from the beginning to the end, shouldn't take precedence over what is out there on the airwaves. Coming to the right conclusion about the topics that John presents is important because getting God's two commands right is crucial for Christians to be able to realize the truth—God is love, and he sent his Son for the world's salvation. Without standing firmly in this court, eternal life will not be attainable.

WHAT TO LOOK FOR AS YOU READ

To follow John's clear logic that is to come, pay attention to the following three areas.

1. Who is born of God?
2. Who is welcome and not welcome in the church?
3. What it means to love one another.

We will have more to say about these topics in our Commentary; however, to prepare for your reading, a quick review of the topics *truth* and *eternal life* will be helpful.

TRUTH

John uses the word *truth* twelve times in the twenty-eight verses of the two upcoming letters. He does this for two reasons, first as a pointer to eternal life and secondly to make a key link to his first letter. When you see the word *truth*, let it register as a reference to God. What is of God is always true. Then let John's specific meaning of *truth* take you beyond its general idea to the following two specifics of truth.

1. *... God gave us eternal life and this life is in his Son ...* (1 Jn 5:11)

    To receive it

2. *... believe in the name of his Son Jesus Christ and love one another...* (1 Jn 3:23).

ETERNAL LIFE

To have eternal life is to live in a state that completely and profoundly *knows* God and his Son Jesus Christ (Jn 17:3). In his first letter, John referred to eternal life twenty-four different ways. In these letters, he refers to eternal life four more ways. Eternal life is when the following occur:

*   When you *know* the truth
*   When the truth abides in you and is with you forever
*   When you walk in the truth
*   When you abide in the doctrine

THE TWO LETTERS ARE COMPLEMENTARY

The two letters are complements to each other in that they focus on two counter-intuitive and difficult choices regarding loving one another. In 2 John, the issue deals with turning away someone who members may know as a neighbor or an associate. In 3 John, the issue is to welcome someone who is a total stranger. Making the loving choice is not always easy, but John will provide the basis for making the correct decision.

CHAPTER 10

2 John
Reject All False Teaching

INTRODUCTION

SYNOPSIS

This letter concerns the challenge those who do not believe in Jesus' name pose to the church. John writes to tell the church not to allow them in to teach their beliefs about who Jesus is. You are going to see how to put the commandment to love one another into action. It will illustrate when the proper response is to say "no."

SPIRAL TEXT

ORIENTATION

We advise getting started by reading the 2 John letter.

2 JOHN (1:1–13)

Walking in the Truth

[1]The elder to the elect lady and her children, whom I love in the truth, and not only I but also all who know the truth, [2]because of the truth which abides in us and will be with us forever, [3d]in truth and love. [3abc]Grace, mercy, and peace will be with us, from God the Father and from Jesus Christ the Father's Son.

[12]Though I have much to write to you, I would rather not use paper and ink, but I hope to come to see you and talk with you face to face, so that our joy may be complete. [13]The children of your elect sister greet you.

Beware of the Deceiver Who Is the Antichrist

[4]I rejoiced greatly to find some of your children walking in the truth, just as we have been commanded by the Father, [7]for many deceivers have gone out into the world. Such a one is the deceiver and the antichrist, men who will not acknowledge the coming of Jesus Christ in the flesh.

[9]Anyone who goes ahead and does not abide in the doctrine of Christ does not have God; he who abides in the doctrine has both the Father and the Son. [10]If any one comes to you and does not bring this doctrine, do not receive him into the house or give him any greeting; [11]for he who greets him shares his wicked work.

Complete Your Journey

[8]Look to yourselves that you may not lose what you have worked for, but may win a full reward.

Love One Another—Keep His Commandments

[5]And now I beg you, lady, not as though I were writing you a new commandment, but the one we have had from the beginning, that we love one another. [6b]This is the commandment, as you have heard from the beginning, that you follow love. [6a]And this is love, that we follow his commandments.

COMMENTARY

WALKING IN THE TRUTH

> **Spiral text:** [1]The elder to the elect lady and her children, whom I love in the truth, and not only I but also all who know the truth, [2]because of the truth which abides in us and will be with us forever, [3d]in truth and love. [3abc]Grace, mercy, and peace will be with us, from God the Father and from Jesus Christ the Father's Son.
>
> [12]Though I have much to write to you, I would rather not use paper and ink, but I hope to come to see you and talk with you face to face, so that our joy may be complete. [13]The children of your elect sister greet you.

JOHN OPENS THE LETTER

John is the elder who directs the letter to the "elect lady and her children." This phrase is a metaphor for the Christian community to whom he writes. The thing to focus on here is not the "lady," but to John's immediate reference to those who *know the truth* (have received eternal life). With this statement, John does three things simultaneously.

1. He immediately draws our attention to eternal life.

    Because of the truth which abides in us and will be with us forever: (2 Jn 1:2)

2. He states <u>all</u> who *know the truth* love this church community. This is the case because those who *know the truth* have eternal life, and, therefore, abide by God's commandment to love. By this, John draws our attention to a core requirement to receive eternal life.

3. John also draws our attention to three benefits of eternal life, which he has not mentioned before. They are grace, mercy, and peace. Each, in its own way, conveys the assurance of receiving salvation through Christ.

a. Grace is God's gift of eternal life.
b. Mercy is Jesus' forgiveness of past sin upon belief and future sin upon confession.
c. Peace arrives when you receive eternal life.

To summarize, John introduces eternal life as the theme and ultimate purpose of this letter by the following methods:

- Drawing our attention to eternal life right off the bat
- Noting love as one of the two core requirements to receive it
- Pointing out what God and his Son will provide to those who have it

This focus on eternal life is a brilliant set-up for the directive that is the message of this letter. John warns the church about a particular kind of deceiver who is a danger to the believers who are still making their way to eternal life. He is the antichrist whose intent is to change people's belief in Jesus.

JOHN'S CONCLUDING REMARK

John uses the phrase *joy may be complete* as another indication of his reason for writing the letter. His goal is for everyone in the community to have eternal life. Only eternal life can bring the complete joy of being with God.

Jesus had the same desire for his disciples when he spoke about them having his complete joy in themselves.

> *"But now I am coming to thee; and these things I speak in the world, that they may have my joy fulfilled in themselves"* (Jn 17:13).

BEWARE OF THE DECEIVER WHO IS THE ANTICHRIST

Spiral text: ⁴I rejoiced greatly to find some of your children walking in the truth, just as we have been commanded by the Father, ⁷for many deceivers have gone out into the world. Such a one is the deceiver and the antichrist, men who will not acknowledge the coming of Jesus Christ in the flesh.

> [9]Anyone who goes ahead and does not abide in the doctrine of Christ does not have God; he who abides in the doctrine has both the Father and the Son. [10]If any one comes to you and does not bring this doctrine, do not receive him into the house or give him any greeting; [11]for he who greets him shares his wicked work.

TRUTH VERSUS DECEPTION

When John rejoices over *some* children walking in the truth, he establishes not all members of the community have received eternal life. Those who have received it follow the Father's commandment completely. Those who have not yet received it are the vulnerable ones. In this letter, John deals with the first part of the Father's commandment—to believe in Jesus' name. They must not waver on this.

When John refers to eternal life here as *walking in the truth*, he is using a new metaphor. He has already referred to eternal life twenty-four other ways. Why did he use a new one? John does this to set up a contrast to emphasize what he has to say about deceivers. They are people who oppose the truth. John also uses this contrast between truth and deception to create a link to his first letter where he introduced the deceivers and provided important information about them.

WHO ARE THE DECEIVERS?

These deceivers are the antichrist. They are people who do not acknowledge the coming of Jesus Christ in the flesh. Worse yet, they are out to sway people away from the true belief in Jesus. The Greek word for deceiver *planos* means someone who is a corrupter, a seducer who misleads.[38]

If those who desire to be with God fall for their teaching, it will be fatal for them. Disbelief in the name of Jesus is a mortal sin.

> ... *This is the antichrist, he who denies the Father and the Son.*
> *No one who denies the Son has the Father* ... (1Jn 2:22–23).

---

[38] http://classic.net.bible.org/strong.php?id=4108.

These deceivers are people who left the church but not necessarily the area where they all live, which means they still might be a neighbor or relative.

They went out from us . . . for if they had been of us, they would have continued with us; but they went out, that it might be plain that they all are not of us (1 Jn 2:19).

If such a deceiver comes knocking on the door to speak or teach, the group might find it hard to turn him down. However, it would be dangerous to let such a person in because those who are closest can be of the greatest influence. John's concern about this is what precipitates this letter.

JOHN'S DIRECTIVE
This church faces the real-world challenge of how to deal with such a deceiver. Today, some might say the church should let him in, in the name of diversity, tolerance, or of loving one's neighbor, but John emphatically advises *not* to. Think about it. These deceivers are out to do something that would take away any chance for eternal life to those who believe them. The loving act is not to allow such a cancer in.

Getting the identity of Jesus right is crucial for eternal life. If Jesus, God's Son, did not come in the flesh, it would mean that he did not really die on the cross or resurrect. This would refute the existence of eternal life itself and the efficacy of God's love; therefore, eliminating the basis for believing Jesus or God. The whole foundation of Christianity rests on the view of Jesus being the Son of God, the Christ who came in the flesh.

COMPLETE YOUR JOURNEY

> **Spiral text:** [8]Look to yourselves that you may not lose what you have worked for, but may win a full reward.

DO NOT GREET THEM
John tells the church do not even give such deceivers greeting. Someone could misconstrue a warm greeting as approval of his or her doctrine. Church leaders have an obligation to protect the vulnerable ones under

their watch, no differently than parents who have an obligation to protect their children. To appear to condone the teaching of the antichrist could cost the eternal life of a member of the family. It would be a mortal sin to let that happen.

When John says *look to yourselves,* he is saying watch out! He explained earlier such a deceiver is not difficult to see.

> *. . . but they went out, that it might be plain that they all are not of us* (1 Jn 2:19).

Letting such a deceiver into the church puts everything at risk. Parents do not let their children play with fire. If church leaders let such a deceiver in, they could ignite a lethal fire.

LOVE ONE ANOTHER—KEEP HIS COMMANDMENTS

> **Spiral text:** ⁵And now I beg you, lady, not as though I were writing you a new commandment, but the one we have had from the beginning, that we love one another. ⁶ᵇThis is the commandment, as you have heard from the beginning, that you follow love. ⁶ᵃAnd this is love, that we follow his commandments.

LOVE IS THE OVERRIDING OBJECTIVE

While the issue that hastened this letter is the part of the Father's commandment that deals with belief, John concludes this letter by returning to love. He actually positions love as the all-encompassing commandment.

> *And this is love, that we follow his commandments . . .* (2 Jn 1:6).

He says to love is to follow both parts of the Father's commandment—to believe in the name of Jesus and to love one another.

> *Beloved, let us love one another; for love is of God, and he who loves is born of God . . . In this the love of God was made manifest*

among us, that God sent his only Son into the world, so that we
might live through him (1Jn 4:7; 9).

John implores the church to love one another; however, in this case, it is necessary to ban someone congregants might know. This is a challenging situation; it could lead to uncomfortable fallout.

It is important to note that John's advice is specific to this issue. He does not generally advocate shunning others; but here, he takes this stand to deal with those who attempt to impose their false beliefs about Jesus on those who are vulnerable. John advocates tough love as the right course—the kind that protects those who are still on their journey to eternal life. In the next letter, however, John portrays a situation that makes it appear he is contradicting himself, but we assure you he is not.

CHAPTER 11

3 John
Love All Your Brethren

INTRODUCTION

SYNOPSIS

This letter concerns the visit of a missionary to an outlying church. The leader refuses to receive such visitors or allow any of his members to welcome them. John has already written a letter to this leader only to learn he does not accept John's authority. Therefore, John now writes to Ga'ius, who is a member of this church and has received the brethren in the past.

ORIENTATION

In his first letter, John identified two phases of the journey to eternal life.

- To become a believer in Jesus' name
- To live a love-based lifestyle

The people in this letter are believers. They have fulfilled the first part of the Father's commandment; however, becoming born of God also depends on how well they love one another.

> *And this is his commandment that we should believe in the name of his Son Jesus Christ and love one another . . .* (1Jn 3:23).

Two of the people in this letter walk in the truth; one is still en route to becoming born of God.

TABLE 11-1. THE PEOPLE IN THE LETTER

PERSON	WHO THEY ARE	BORN-OF-GOD STATUS
Ga'ius	A member of the church whom John writes to	Is born of God/walks in the truth
Deme'trius	The missionary coming to visit the church	Is born of God/walks in the truth
Diot'rephes	The leader of the church	En route, not born of God

The commandment that is the focus of this letter is that of loving a brother, which Diot'rephes is failing to do.

And this commandment we have from him, that he who loves God should love his brother also (1Jn 4:21).

SPIRAL TEXT

ORIENTATION

We advise getting started with an overview. Read the letter as it is depicted below.

3 JOHN (1:1–15)

Introduction

[1]The elder to the beloved Ga'ius; whom I love in the truth. [2b]I know that it is well with your soul. [2a]Beloved, I pray that all may go well with you and that you may be in health.

[13]I had much to write to you, but I would rather not write with pen and ink; [14]I hope to see you soon, and we will talk together face to face. [15]Peace be to you. The friends greet you. Greet the friends, every one of them by name.

Gaius Renders Service to the Brethren

[3]For I greatly rejoiced when some of the brethren arrived and testified to the truth of your life, as indeed you do follow the truth. [5]Beloved, it is a loyal thing you do when you render any service to the brethren, [6a]especially to strangers, who have testified to your love before the church. [4]No greater joy can I have than this, to hear that my children follow the truth.

[8]So we ought to support such men, that we may be fellow workers in the truth. [6bc]You will do well to send them on their journey as befits God's service. [7]For they have set out for his sake and have accepted nothing from the heathen.

[12]Deme'trius has testimony from everyone, and from the truth itself; I testify to him too, and you know my testimony is true.

Diot'rephes Doesn't Welcome the Brethren

[9]I have written something to the church; but Diot'rephes, who likes to put himself first, does not accept my authority. [10b]And not content with that, he refuses himself to welcome the brethren, [10d]and puts them out of the church [10c]and also stops those that want to welcome them. [10a]So if I come, I will bring up what he is doing, prating against me with evil words.

Imitate Good

[11a]Beloved, do not imitate evil ([11c]he who does evil has not seen God) [11b]but imitate good. He who does good is of God.

COMMENTARY

INTRODUCTION

Spiral text: [1]The elder to the beloved Ga'ius; whom I love in the truth. [2b]I know that it is well with your soul. [2a]Beloved, I pray that all may go well with you and that you may be in health.

[13]I had much to write to you, but I would rather not write with pen and ink; [14]I hope to see you soon, and we will talk together face to face. [15]Peace be to you. The friends greet you. Greet the friends, every one of them by name.

JOHN OPENS THE LETTER

Here, we have the standard opening and closing of a letter by John who identifies himself as the elder. He directs this letter to Ga'ius, a member of an outlying church. Once again, he draws our attention to eternal life with his acknowledgment that all is well with Ga'ius' soul. This leads to two questions.

- How does John know this?
- Why is he bringing it up, right up front?

We will learn the answers in the next section, but before we go there, let's look at the next passage.

JOHN'S MENTION OF "FRIENDS"

In his concluding remarks, John mentions the mutual greeting of friends from community to community, which looks like standard protocol; however, there is something more to it. This use of the word *friends* is a connection to what Jesus said to the disciples about friends that draws our attention to the very issue John will deal with in this letter, that of loving one another.

"You are my friends if you do what I command you . . . I have called you friends, for all that I have heard from my Father I have

made known to you . . . This I command you, to love one another" (Jn 15:14–15; 17).

This letter brings to light one of the challenges of loving one another that is still before us to this day—how to do what you think is right when someone in authority opposes it.

GA'IUS RENDERS SERVICE TO THE BRETHREN

Spiral text: [3]For I greatly rejoiced when some of the brethren arrived and testified to the truth of your life as indeed you do <u>walk</u> in the truth. [5]Beloved, it is a loyal thing you do when you render any service to the brethren, [6a]especially to strangers, who have *testified to your love* before the church. [4]No greater joy can I have than this, to hear that my children <u>walk in</u> the truth.

[8]So we ought to support such men, that we may be fellow workers in the truth. [6bc]You will do well to send them on their journey as befits God's service. [7]For they have set out for his sake and have accepted nothing from the heathen.

[12]Deme'trius has testimony from everyone, and from the truth itself; I testify to him too, and you know my testimony is true.

WHO IS GA'IUS

John knows Ga'ius is born of God because he was told so by some of the brethren who had traveled to Ga'ius' community. John commends Ga'ius for his faithfulness to God's command to love fellow Christians. What makes Ga'ius' love of brother notable is he rendered service to brethren who were strangers and apparently he did it in face of opposition from the leader of his church.

And this commandment we have from him, that he who loves God should love his brother also (1Jn 4:21).

While people may love relatives, acquaintances, or members of their church whom they personally know, this command expands those one should love beyond those close to home. Jesus came to save the world, and this command states the necessity to love all who are part of God's new family, even total strangers.

JOHN TELLS GA´IUS TO SUPPORT THE MISSIONARIES

John encourages Ga´ius to support workers of the truth, but why do this when Ga´ius has already demonstrated that this is what he does? John has a specific situation in mind, which is the upcoming visit of Deme'trius. John identifies him as a worker in the truth, who is a fellow brother in God's family.

> *. . . I testify to him too and you know my testimony is true* (2 Jn 1:12).

With this kind of character reference, what stands in the way of his welcome? Why is John writing to a member of the church about this and not to the leader?

DIOT'REPHES DOES NOT WELCOME THE BRETHREN

> **Spiral text:** [9]I have written something to the church; but Diot'rephes, who likes to put himself first, does not accept my authority. [10b]And not content with that, he refuses himself to welcome the brethren, [10d]and puts them out of the church [10c]and also stops those that want to welcome them. [10a]So if I come, I will bring up what he is doing, prating against me with evil words.

WHO IS DIOT'REPHES?

Diot'rephes is the leader of this community. He is a believer, still on the journey to becoming born of God. He is vulnerable to committing non-loving acts, which he is doing in three cases.

- Not responding in a loving manner to John who is Jesus' beloved disciple who walks in the truth
- Not welcoming strangers who walk in the truth

- Not allowing members of his church to welcome strangers who walk in the truth

We have a situation where the church leader is misguided. John says he will deal with this when he is there in person; however, what should people do in the meantime?

IMITATE GOOD

> **Spiral text:** [11a]Beloved, do not imitate evil ([11c]he who does evil has not seen God) [11b]but imitate good. He who does good is of God.

THE CRUX OF THE LETTER

John has asked Ga'ius a church member, to welcome Deme'trius when he arrives at the church. John is asking Ga'ius to override the authority of the leader in order to do the loving act. The crux of this letter is do what you know is right, which in this case is to not follow (imitate) evil.

He who loves his brother abides in the light, and in it there is no cause for stumbling (1Jn 2:10).

Ga'ius knows that the right thing to do is to welcome the brethren; he has done it before. John is asking him to say "yes" to love again, which means Ga'ius must say "no" to his misguided leader. Diot'rephes, who is not born of God, has fallen prey to evil.

2 JOHN & 3 JOHN
CONCLUSION

IT IS OKAY TO SAY "NO"

Both 2 John and 3 John take the command to love out to the challenges of the real world. Both present examples of the need to seize the opportunity to make the true loving choice in spite of potential negative fallout. The world is full of such choice points. John is calling for people to shuck their passivity and be vigorous and courageous warriors for love.

> *Little children, let us not love in word or speech but in deed and in truth* (1Jn 3:18).

In 2 John, it was necessary to say "no" to those who would try to dissuade believers from Jesus. The loving action was to protect the vulnerable and bar the deceivers' admittance to the church. 3 John illustrates the necessity to not follow a leader who is not allowing the loving action of welcoming a brother to take place.

When read in the traditional way, the two letters appear to contradict each other. In one, John's advice is to turn someone away from the church; in the other, John advises welcoming someone. However, the spiral text reveals that love unifies these two letters and that in the context of the higher calling, it is appropriate to reject any opposition to it.

Spiral Text Explained

"The content does not lie behind the form but within it. Whoever is not capable of seeing and 'reading' the form will fail to perceive the content."

—Hans Urs von Balthasar, one of the most significant theologians of the twentieth century

APPENDIX A

Introduction to
Spiral Text

THE PURPOSE OF THIS APPENDIX

In chapter 1, we explained how research into the literary structure of the Bible has made it possible to more easily and accurately understand John's letters. To take advantage of this research, we converted the scriptural text of all three of John's letters into spiral form so that you could read them with the same ease, fluidity, and comprehensibility as his 1ˢᵗ century listeners had. The purpose of this appendix is to explain how we formulated this spiral text.

OUR APPROACH

We developed our spiral text protocols from discoveries biblical scholars have written about over the last fifty years. This field is relatively new in the 2,000-year schema of biblical scholarship and is bringing exciting breakthroughs in enhanced understanding of Scripture.

After a slow start beginning in the late nineteenth century, rhetorical criticism of the Bible received new impetus in 1968, when James Muilenburg president of the Society of Biblical Literature encouraged scholars to look more seriously at the structural patterns of the Bible.[39] Unfortunately, his encouragement came with a complication—1ˢᵗ century writers never formally wrote out their structures. These "invisible" structures could only be decoded through their repetitive words, sounds, and concepts.

---

[39] David A. Dorsey, *The Literary Structure of the Old Testament, A Commentary on Genesis–Malachi* (Grand Rapids, MI: Baker Books, 1999) 20.

WHO IS THIS APPENDIX FOR?

We will do our best to keep our explanations of chiastic structures simple, but structural analysis is a technical process with its own specialized lexicon. Please understand the material in this appendix is *not* necessary for those who simply wish to read John's letters. The spiral text we have provided in this book will suffice for that. This appendix is intended for those who want to dig into the mechanical details of the formulation of spiral text.

DEFINITION OF SPIRAL TEXT AS IT PERTAINS TO JOHN'S WRITINGS

Spiral text is scriptural text arranged according to the chiastic structuring techniques John used in his writings. Spiral text has the look and feel of the text you would see in your Bible. The words are the same; however, their sequence is not strictly in linear order. Instead, passages are sequenced according to their relationship with other passages that mutually reside within a structure.

THE PURPOSE OF SPIRAL TEXT

Spiral text puts modern readers on the "same page" as 1st century listeners. Is this important? The answer is an emphatic yes! It gives modern readers access to the same context John's 1st century listeners used to understand and live out his message. Spiral text provides clarity, accuracy, and coherence for the modern reader that a linear reading cannot provide.

AN INTRODUCTION TO THE FORMULATION OF SPIRAL TEXT

In Chapter 1, we used Matthew 7:6 to show how chiastic structure alleviates the confusion about whether the dogs or swine attack. We refer to this verse again to lead into John's three-part, multi-layered structures that are the basis for the spiral text used in this book.

The structural labels of Matthew 7:6 shown below indicate how 1st century listeners would have connected the outer passages **A** with **A '** and the interior passages **B** with **B '** to create a different thought pattern than what modern readers take away from the passage.

FIGURE A–1. MATTHEW 7:6 IN CHIASTIC STRUCTURAL FORM

> **A** *Do not give dogs what is holy*
> **B** *and do not throw your pearls before swine,*
> **B'** *lest they trample them under foot*
> **A'** *and turn to attack you (Mt 7:6).*

First-century Semites had been listening to chiastic structures this way for thousands of years.[40] Because John's letters are full of them, modern readers who have not been trained to read or listen for first/last chiastic pairings, have a problem. Spiral text solves this by arranging the text so modern readers can read scriptural text the same way 1st century listeners heard and comprehended it.

THE BIRTH OF SPIRAL TEXT

Look at the spiral text of Mathew 7:6 below. The passages go from the first passage **A** (**7:6a**) to the parallel complement **A'** (**7:6d**), and finishes with **B** (**7:6b**) followed by **B'** (**7:6c**).

FIGURE A–2. MATTHEW 7:6 IN SPIRAL FORM

> **Spiral text:** 7:6a *Do not give dogs what is holy;* 7:6d *[they] turn to attack you;* 7:6b *and do not throw your pearls before swine,* 7:6c *lest they trample them under foot.*

The main thrust of spiral text is to bring parallel passages together, which is what we did here. The **A'** passage was moved up to follow the **A** passage. This example makes the reason for the enhanced coherence quite clear. Writers like Matthew and John used the second parallel passage to elaborate upon and explain the idea presented in the first parallel passage.

---

[40] Isaac Mendelsohn, editor, *Religions of the Ancient Near East: Sumero-Akkadian Religious Texts and Ugaritic Epics.* (Liberal Arts Press, 1955).

In this case, the first parallel **A** is a directive; the second parallel **A′** explains the reason for it. If you give dogs what is holy, they will attack you. Modern readers look for this kind of thought completion right after a thought is initiated. When there is a gap, as frequently occurs in chiastic structures, the second parallel or *parallel complement* as it is called, can be easily overlooked, which leads to confusion and incorrect conclusions. Spiral text places parallel passages next to each other to close the gap.

NOW WE ARE READY TO LOOK AT JOHN'S STRUCTURES

John's chiastic structures typically add a third element to their formation— a point of prominence, which is the key point. John typically used parallel passages to bookend the point of prominence. We will use the first seven verses of 1 John to illustrate this kind of structural formation and explain the following:

- The functions of each element of John's three-part chiastic structure.
- The four ways John varied his chiastic structures.
- How to detect John's chiastic structures by the repetition of words, sounds, and concepts.
- The protocol for creating spiral text from John's chiastic structures.

The structural configurations we are about to show you will reveal John's amazing facility with language and structure. Scholars have called him genius[41] and masterful.[42] Your exposure to the structures of these seven verses alone may lead you to the same conclusion.

REPETITIVE WORDS ARE KEY TO IDENTIFYING JOHN'S STRUCTURES

John used the repetition of three words to organize what he had to say in the seven verses in Part **A** of this letter.

Heard	Seen	Fellowship

---

[41] Peter F. Ellis, *The Genius of John* (The Liturgical Press, 1984) 1.

[42] John J. Gerhard, S.J., *The Miraculous Parallelisms of John*, (The Orlando Truth, Inc., 2006) 29.

We will start by highlighting the repetition of these three words in the linear text of Part **A**.

1 JOHN (1:1-7) PART A IN LINEAR ORDER

> [1:1a] That which was from the beginning, [1:1b] which we **have heard**, [1:1c] which we **have seen** with our eyes, which we have looked upon and touched with our hands, concerning the word of life. [2a] the life was made manifest, [2b] and we **saw** it, and testify to it, and proclaim to you the eternal life, [2c] which was with the Father and was made manifest to us [3a] that which we **have seen and heard** we proclaim also to you, [3b] so that you may have **fellowship** with us [3c] and our **fellowship** is with the Father and with his Son Jesus Christ. [4] And we are writing this that our joy may be complete [1:5a] This is the message we **have heard** from him and announce to you, that God is light and in him is no darkness at all. [6] If we say **we have fellowship** with him while we walk in darkness, we lie and do not live according to the truth; [7a] but if we walk in the light, as he is in the light, **we have fellowship** with one another, [7b] and the blood of Jesus his Son cleanses us from all sin.

The chart below provides a summary view of where the key repetitive words are located. For 1st century listeners, these words acted like magnets pulling them from verse 1:1 to verse 1:3 and on to verse 1:7, the outer boundary of Part **A**. This kind of magnetic effect of same words drawing the listener to another passage is parallelism at work.

TABLE A-1. REPETITIVE WORD ANALYSIS 1 JOHN 1:1-7

BLOCK	VERSE(S)	REPETITIVE WORDS		
1	1:1	Heard	Seen	
2	1:2		Saw	
3	1:3–7	Heard	Seen	Fellowship

THE NEXT STEP IS TO ASCERTAIN THE CHIASTIC STRUCTURES

Identifying the chiastic structures that arise from parallelism is the necessary intermediate step in the development of spiral text; however, it is *not* a necessary step for users of spiral text. For example, people who want to drive a car need only know how to start the ignition and shift the gear from park to drive. They do not need to understand how the engine works. You could liken this explanation of chiastic structure to explaining how a car's engine works. If you are someone who wants to understand what is under the hood, please read on!

JOHN'S TYPICAL THREE-PART CHIASTIC STRUCTURE

John's typical chiastic structure is like a hamburger. The two parallel passages are like the two sides of a bun that hold a hamburger patty, which is the point of prominence, labeled **b** below. John introduces a topic with the first usage of a key word in the first parallel passage **a**; then he provides more information about the topic in the word's second usage, in the parallel complement **a´**.

The label of a parallel complement is always the same letter used for the first parallel passage with the addition of a prime symbol. The word *complement* means to complete, which is what John does in the parallel complement. He completes what he wants his readers to know about the topic by elaborating on it, explaining it, or extending it.

FIGURE A-3. THREE PARTS OF JOHN'S TYPICAL CHIASTIC STRUCTURE

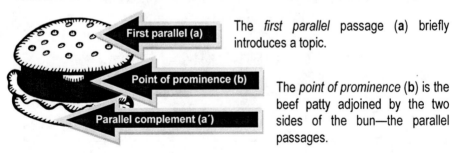

The *first parallel* passage **(a)** briefly introduces a topic.

The *point of prominence* **(b)** is the beef patty adjoined by the two sides of the bun—the parallel passages.

John provides further elucidation of the original topic in the *parallel complement* **(a´)**.

THE CHIASTIC LABELS OF VERSES 1:1–7

In the table below, verses 1:1–7 are in linear verse order, but you will be able to determine their structural function by the labels on the left **a: b: a′**.

1. The first letter **a** introduces a topic.
2. The same letter with a prime symbol **a′** elaborates on a topic.
3. The different letter **b** is the point of prominence—the <u>key point</u>.

Notice in **a**, how John starts by <u>introducing</u> the main topic—the word of life. The parallel complement **a′** <u>explains</u> what John wants you to know about it. He proclaims the word of life to his audience so they can have fellowship with the Father and his Son. In the point of prominence **b**, John makes the awesome announcement—God is restoring eternal life. This is the <u>ultimate</u> <u>message</u> and the key point of the entire letter.

TABLE A-2. 1 JOHN 1:1-7 TEXT IN LINEAR ORDER WITH CHIASTIC LABELS

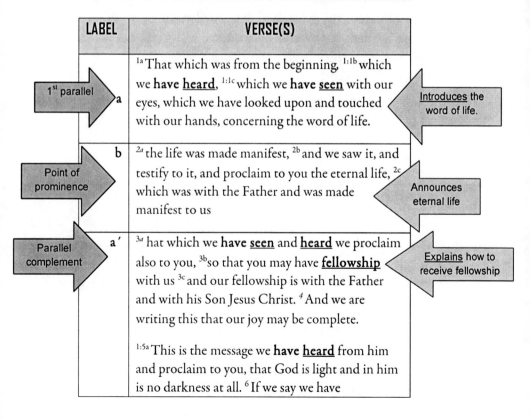

LABEL		VERSE(S)
1st parallel	a	¹ᵃ That which was from the beginning, ¹:¹ᵇ which we **have** <u>**heard**</u>, ¹:¹ᶜ which we **have** <u>**seen**</u> with our eyes, which we have looked upon and touched with our hands, concerning the word of life. _Introduces the word of life._
Point of prominence	b	²ᵃ the life was made manifest, ²ᵇ and we saw it, and testify to it, and proclaim to you the eternal life, ²ᶜ which was with the Father and was made manifest to us _Announces eternal life_
Parallel complement	a′	³ᵃ hat which we **have** <u>**seen**</u> and <u>**heard**</u> we proclaim also to you, ³ᵇ so that you may have **fellowship** with us ³ᶜ and our fellowship is with the Father and with his Son Jesus Christ. ⁴ And we are writing this that our joy may be complete. _Explains how to receive fellowship_ ¹:⁵ᵃ This is the message we **have** <u>**heard**</u> from him and proclaim to you, that God is light and in him is no darkness at all. ⁶ If we say we have

LABEL	VERSE(S)
	fellowship with him while we walk in darkness, we lie and do not live according to the truth; [7a] but if we walk in the light, as he is in the light, we have **fellowship** with one another, [7b] and the blood of Jesus his Son cleanses us from all sin.

The pivotal step in the development of spiral text is to label each block of linear text according to its chiastic function because the labels define the sequence of the verses in spiral text.

SPIRAL READING SEQUENCE OF VERSES 1:1–7

We listed the labels in the table below in the order the spiral text of 1:1–7 will be formulated. The parallel pairs are first and the point of prominence is last. The guideline for spiral text is to start the list the passages with those labeled in the earliest alphabetic occurrence and progress to the last alphabetic occurrence, which in this case is **a: a′: b.**

TABLE A-3. SPIRAL TEXT SEQUENCE 1 JOHN 1:1-7

LABEL	VERSE(S)	FUNCTION	REPETITIVE WORDS
a	1:1	1st Parallel	Heard and seen
a′	1:3-7	Parallel complement	Seen, heard and fellowship
b	1:2	Point of prominence	Saw

WHERE WE ARE NOW

This "look under the hood" delivered the first cut of blocks of text that could become spiral text by the labeling in the chart on the previous page, but it is *not* our end point. We need to determine whether there are deeper layers of structure that John intended for his 1st century audience to hear.

To proceed, we will look for more parallelism. There are three ways to spot it.

THREE TYPES OF PARALLEL RELATIONSHIPS

Thus far, we have emphasized word repetition of either the same or opposite words to identify parallelism, but there is another method. Robert Lowth, Lord Bishop of London included it when he presented the three types of parallel relationships in his address at Oxford in 1753.[43]

TABLE A-4. THREE TYPES OF PARALLEL RELATIONSHIPS

#	TYPE	FUNCTION	REPETITION
1.	Synthetic	Completes the thought that was first introduced	Not typical
2.	Synonymous	Repeats the topic and elaborates on it	Most used
3.	Antithetic	Contrasts the topic	Generally used

We will provide examples from the verses 1:1–7 to illustrate how each of these parallel types work. Only when you identify the parallel passages can you create the chiastic structures with the labels necessary for the formation of spiral text. The examples we are about to show you are the structures that led to the spiral text you read in Chapter 3. We will start with the synthetic type found in verse 1:1. It links two passages without any word repetition.

THE SYNTHETIC TYPE

The synthetic type of parallelism is *not* as obvious a connecting device, as word repetition is, but it was clearly evident to those in the 1st century. Synthetic parallelism is based on the idea of synthesis; it combines the elements of a parallel pair to create one complete idea. To see it at work, start by reading verse 1:1 below in its linear order.

---

[43] Nils Wilhelm Lund, *Chiasmus in the New Testament: A Study in the Form and Function of Chiastic Structures* (Peabody MA, Hendrickson Publishers, reprinted 1992) 36.

1 JOHN 1:1 IN LINEAR ORDER

> [1a] That which *was from the beginning,* [1:1b] which we have heard, [1:1c] which we have seen with our eyes, which we have looked upon and touched with our hands, *concerning the word of life.*

This verse contains words heard and seen that were used to form parallel relationships with verses 1:3–7 earlier, but now, our objective is to develop the chiastic structure of verse 1:1 itself; therefore, these words will not play into our consideration.

With this in mind, let's look at how John sets up his synthetic parallelism. When you read the opening passage, did you wonder what was *from the beginning?* If you think of Genesis, there are many possibilities which have been much debated, but you don't have to wonder about this. John immediately clears this up in the parallel complement.

THE SYNTHETIC TYPE AT WORK

In the first parallel passage **aa** below, John brings up the topic, *that which was from the beginning.* In the parallel complement **aa′**, he tells us it is the word of life. There is *no* word repetition here. John synthesizes two separate topics to form one idea—the word of life is what was with God from the beginning.

In this light, consider the power of the point of prominence **bb** when it follows these two parallel passages as it does, in spiral text. The parallel passages provide the context for John's statement that he and the disciples heard, saw, and touched the word of life—they touched the risen Son of God!

TABLE A–5. STRUCTURE OF 1 JOHN 1:1 WITH SYNTHETIC PARALLEL ELEMENTS

LABEL	SCRIPTURAL PASSAGE	CHIASTIC FUNCTION
aa	[1:1a] That which was from the beginning,	**First parallel**
bb	[1:1b] Which we have heard, which we have seen with our eyes, which we have looked upon and touched with our hands	**Point of prominence**
aa′	[1:1c] concerning the word of life	**Parallel complement**

Notice these labels are double letters. This is because they signify a deeper layer of structure. We will discuss structural layers ahead, but what is important to note, is the system of starting with the earliest letter in the alphabet and going forward still holds as the guideline for formulating the sequence of spiral text.

THE SPIRAL TEXT OF 1 JOHN 1:1

Spiral text: [1:1a] That which was from the beginning, [1:1c] concerning the word of life, [1:1b] which we have heard, which we have seen with our eyes, which we have looked upon and touched with our hands.

THE SYNONYMOUS TYPE

Synonymous parallelism is based on the repetition of words and /or sounds. The repetition of *was made manifest* is the basis for a synonymous parallel relationship in verse 1:2. Read verse 1:2 below to see it at work.

1 JOHN 1:2 IN LINEAR ORDER

[1:2] The life **was made manifest**, and we saw it, and testify to it, and proclaim to you the eternal life, which was with the Father and **was made manifest** to us.

THE SYNONYMOUS TYPE AT WORK

In the first parallel passage **aa** below, John states the life *was made manifest.* Why does he want you to know this; what is his point? The parallel complement **aa'** answers. John says something more about the original topic that is the point <u>he</u> wants to make—the life that *was made manifest* to John and the disciples was with the Father.

This repetition in the parallel complement provides credibility for John's testimony in the point of prominence **bb** and magnifies the power of John's proclamation of eternal life, which is the theme of the letter.

TABLE A–6. THE STRUCTURE OF 1 JOHN 1:2 WITH SYNONYMOUS PARALLEL ELEMENTS

LABEL	SCRIPTURAL PASSAGE	CHIASTIC FUNCTION
aa	²ᵃ the life *was made manifest,*	First parallel
bb	²ᵇ we saw it, and testify to it, and proclaim to you the eternal life	Point of prominence
aa'	²:ᶜ which was with the Father and *was made manifest* to us	Parallel complement

SPIRAL TEXT (1 JOHN 1:2)

Spiral text: ¹:²ᵃ The life was made manifest, ²ᶜ which was with the Father and was made manifest to us. ²ᵇ We saw it and testify to it, and proclaim to you the eternal life.

THE ANTITHETIC TYPE

The third type of parallel relationship is called *antithetic* because the two parallel passages are in contrast to each other. You may or may *not* see words repeated, but you will see emphasis on their dissimilarity. In verses 1:6–7, which we will discuss further ahead, John will contrast a brother who is in the light and has fellowship with God with one who walks in the darkness and does *not* have fellowship with God.

JOHN'S STYLISTIC VARIATIONS

When musical composers repeat material by changing its melody, rhythm, or orchestration, the technique is called variation. John uses variation in his writing too. He makes his compositions more effective and interesting four ways. He varies:

1. The way the parallel passages relate to each other—they can be in a synthetic, synonymous, or antithetic relationship.
2. The location of the point of prominence in a structure—it can be at the top, bottom, center, or non-existent.
3. The size of a chiastic structure, which is based on the number of parallel pairs contained within it and whether it has a point or prominence.
4. The number of layers of structures within a structure.

In the preceding pages, we described how John varied the parallelism in his chiastic structures. Next, we will look at the way John changes the location of the point of prominence within his structures.

THE POINT OF PROMINENCE IS *NOT* ALWAYS IN THE CENTER

Thus far, you have only seen the point of prominence appear between the parallel passages in the center of a structure (like a beef patty between the hamburger buns). In the example below, the point of prominence appears at the beginning of the structure before the parallel passages.

Because it states the structure's main idea first and is followed by two parallel passages that provide the specifics about the idea, this chiastic structure is called a *general to specific* type.

TABLE A-7. STRUCTURE WITH POINT OF PROMINENCE FIRST (1 JOHN 1:3)

LABEL	SCRIPTURAL PASSAGE	CHIASTIC FUNCTION
aa	[3a] That which we have seen and heard we proclaim also to you	**Point of prominence**
bb	[3b] so that you may have fellowship with us	**First parallel**
bb'	[3c] and our **fellowship** is with the Father and with his Son Jesus Christ	**Parallel complement**

Notice the point of prominence is labeled with the earliest letter in the alphabet **aa**. The parallel passages follow with the next alphabetic letter **bb** and **bb'**. In this case, the labels lead to spiral text that is linear not spiral.

SPIRAL TEXT (1 JOHN 1:3)

Spiral text: [3] That which we have seen and heard we proclaim also to you so that you may have fellowship with us, and our fellowship is with the Father and with his Son Jesus Christ.

THE VALUE OF A CHIASTIC STRUCTURE WITH A LINEAR SEQUENCE

Since the spiral reading of 1:3 is the same as you would read in the Bible, why go to the trouble to convert it into spiral text? The benefits are two-fold—enhanced clarity and contribution to the whole.

This type of structure helped the 1st century listeners comprehend what John wished to emphasize because the point of prominence is in the first position. Its additional contribution is as a building block. Because it contains the repetitive words *seen*, *heard*, and *fellowship*, it provides linkage to verses 1:1 and 1:5–7. Like a picture puzzle, John's message wouldn't be evident if any pieces were missing. Even if this building block is arranged linearly, it is needed.

THE THIRD VARIATION IS TO CHANGE THE SIZE OF A STRUCTURE

Not all of John's structures are three parts. His base layer structures typically range from three to five parts, but the structure shown below is four parts. John composed it with a second set of parallel passages and did not include a point of prominence.

TABLE A-8. 4-PART NO POINT OF PROMINENCE CHIASTIC STRUCTURE (1 JOHN 1:5-7)

LABEL	SCRIPTURAL PASSAGE	CHIASTIC FUNCTION
aa	[5] This is the message we *have heard from him* and *proclaim to you,* that God is light and in him is no darkness at all	First parallel
bb	[6] *If we say we have fellowship with him while we walk in darkness,* we lie and do not live according to the truth	First parallel
bb′	[7a] but *if we walk in the light* as he is in the light, we have *fellowship with him*	Parallel complement
aa′	[7b] and the blood of Jesus his *Son* cleanses us from all sin	Parallel complement

The **aa** and **aa′** parallel pair is synthetic. The first parallel **aa** sets up the fact God is complete light (sinless). The parallel complement **aa′** states Jesus cleanses humans of their sin (darkness), so they can come into the light and be in fellowship with God. The two passages create a synthesis—God and humans can come together through Jesus' cleansing activities.

The **bb** and **bb′** pair is antithetic. John contrasts who has fellowship with who does not.

SPIRAL TEXT (1 JOHN 1:5–7)

Spiral text: [5] This is the message we have heard from him and proclaim to you, that God is light and in him is no darkness at all [7c]and the blood of Jesus his Son cleanses us from all sin.

[6] If we say we have fellowship with him while we walk in darkness, we lie and do not live according to the truth; [7ab]but if we walk in the light as he is in the light, we have fellowship with him.

THE FOURTH VARIATION DEALS WITH LAYERS OF STRUCTURE

Thus far, we have looked at individual chiastic structures that comprise the first seven verses of 1 John. They function as a hierarchical organization chart. Each one serves as a layer in the multi-layered structure of Part **A**.

SPIRAL TEXT OF PART A (1 JOHN 1:1–7)

Fellowship with God

Spiral text: [1:1a] That which was from the beginning, [1c]concerning the word of life, [1b]which we **have heard**, which we **have seen** with our eyes, which we have looked upon and touched with our hands. [1:3] That which we **have seen and heard** we proclaim also to you so that you may have **fellowship** with us, and our **fellowship** is with the Father and with his Son Jesus Christ.

Walk in the Light

[1:5] This is the message we **have heard** from him and proclaim to you, that God is light and in him is no darkness at all [7b]and the blood of Jesus his Son cleanses us from all sin.

[1:6] If we say we have **fellowship** with him while we walk in darkness, we lie and do not live according to the truth; [7a]but if we walk in the light as he is in the light, we have **fellowship** with him.

> ## The Gift of Eternal Life
> [4] And we are writing this that your joy may be complete. [1:2a]The life was made manifest, [2c]which was with the Father and was made manifest to us. [2b]We **saw** it and testify to it, and proclaim to you the eternal life.

WHAT IS NEXT?

John closes Part **A** by powerfully stating he and the disciples saw *the eternal life*—they testify to it and proclaim it, but what do they proclaim? As we discussed earlier, the parallel complement answers these kinds of questions by elaborating on what John introduced in the first parallel (Part **A**). This is what you will find in Part **A**′ (5:18-21). It picks up with what John and the disciples personally know about eternal life. Let us look at this beautiful completion. Its implications are stunning.

SPIRAL TEXT OF PART A′ (1 JOHN 5:18–21)

> ## The Benefits of Eternal Life
> **Spiral text:** [5:18a]We **know** that any one born of God does not sin, [19]we **know** that we are of God, and the whole world is in the power of the evil one; [18b]but he who was born of God keeps him, and the evil one does not touch him. [20]And we **know** that the Son of God has come and has given us understanding, to **know** him who is true; and we are in him who is true, in his Son Jesus Christ. This is the true God and eternal life.

> ## The Challenge
> [5:21]Little children, keep yourselves from idols.

WHY DIDN'T JOHN JUST WRITE IN SPIRAL FORM?

The process of constructing spiral text is intricate and completely dependent on auditory cues. John's word, sound, and concept repetition unlocks a very sophisticated and logical way to communicate to an aural audience. The protocol we have described makes it possible to see what has been has been hidden from view for over a thousand years. This is a very significant breakthrough!

People sometimes ask why John didn't just write in spiral text. The answer is simple—John wrote in the oral tradition of his day for people who needed repetition to mentally assemble what he had to say. While modern writers no longer need to split their thoughts in half and repeat their words the way John did, modern readers do need a bridge across the 2,000 year gap in writing. Spiral text is the bridge. With spiral text, modern readers have the opportunity to read John as 1st century listeners heard and comprehended his sacred message without having to change the way they read.

Appendix B

Spiral Text Portrayed

The Chiastic Structures of John's Letters

INTRODUCTION

PURPOSE OF THIS APPENDIX
The purpose of this appendix is to provide the technical view of the chiastic structural elements of John's three letters. A chiastic structure is like a motor engine. A technician looks under the hood of a car to see how its engine converts potential energy into actual energy to get a car moving. Chiastic structures also reside "under the hood" in that they are embedded within the scriptural text we read today. A chiastic structure is also like an engine, because it too is a conversion mechanism. It converts John's words from linear to spiral form in order to "move" today's readers.

JOHN'S EXTENSIVE USE OF CHIASTIC STRUCTURE
The existence of chiastic structures may be news today, but it wasn't news in the 1st century. There is too much archeological evidence of its existence to think otherwise. Because it was commonly used to communicate with an aural audience, we can say John did *not* sprinkle his chiastic structures here and there. His letters are complete chiastic structures.

THE CHIASTIC STRUCTURE OF JOHN'S FIRST LETTER
We will provide an overview of the mega chiastic structure of John's first letter. It is large with many intricate substructures, which are shown in complete detail in the pages that follow. We will focus on John's megastructure and its message here, to provide the theological context for these structures.

THE OVERALL CHIASTIC STRUCTURE OF 1 JOHN

You can think of this megastructure as the "engine" that converts linear text to spiral form. We are excited to share it with you, because it takes seeing it at it high level to clearly realize the ultimate message of John's letters. His purpose was to tell his community of believers how to receive eternal life. What he says is as important for Christians today as it was in the 1st century. He speaks to the fundamentals of Christianity.

It will important to note several things in the megastructure of 1 John shown below.

- This letter is a five-part chiastic structure **A, B, C, B′ A′** containing two sets of parallel pairs (**A / A′** and **B / B′**) and one point of prominence (**C**).
- Its 105 verses are listed in linear order.
- The labels depict the chiastic organization of the letter, which provide the basis for the formulation of its spiral text.

THE MEGASTRUCTURE

The outer labels on the left **A, B, C, B′, A′** define the five major parts of the first letter. In Appendix A, we discussed the details of Part **A** of this structure showing how its labels provided the sequence for spiral reading by starting with the label with the first alphabetic occurrence and reading everything there before moving forward to the other labels. The detailed structures that follow may have as many as five layers, yet they all follow this protocol.

TABLE B-1. CHIASTIC STRUCTURE OF 1 JOHN

1 JOHN (CHAPTERS 1–5)		
Labels		**Verses**
A		1:1–7
B	a	1:8–2:2
	b	2:3–11
	a′	2:12–28
C		**2:29–3:10**
B′	a	3:11–4:6
	b	4:7–5:3
	c	5:4–5
	b′	5:6–13
	a′	5:14–17
A′		5:18–21

THE MESSAGE OF THE MEGASTRUCTURE

When you look at what John says in spiral order, the logic of the letter's message comes through loud and clear—John announces eternal life; he tells you how to receive it, and he tells you the choice is yours.

1. The first parallel pair (**A/A′**) in 11 verses, does three things:

   - Announces God's gift of eternal life
   - Identifies the role of Jesus
   - States what humans need to do to receive eternal life

2. The 2ⁿᵈ parallel pair (**B/B′**) in 85 verses, presents:

- Specifically how Jesus supports the believing community
- The Father's new commandment to believe and love
- Explicit instructions in how to receive eternal life

3. The point of prominence (**C**) in 11 verses synthesizes John's entire message to one choice—purify and have eternal life with God or sin and die.

DETAILED CHIASTIC STRUCTURES

PROCLAMATION OF ETERNAL LIFE

			1 John: Segment A (1:1–7)
a	**aa**		1:1aThat which was from the beginning,
	bb		1:1bWhich we *have heard*, which we *have seen* with our eyes, which we have looked upon and touched with our hands
	a′		1:1cconcerning the word of life
b	**aa**		2athe life *was made manifest*,
	bb		2b*and we saw it*, and testify to it, and *proclaim to you the eternal life*,
	aa′		2c which was with the Father and *was made manifest* to us
a′	**aa**	**X**	3a*that which we have seen and heard* we proclaim also to you,
		Y	3bso that you *may have fellowship with* us;
		Y′	3cand *our fellowship is* with the Father and with his Son Jesus Christ.
	bb		4And we are writing this that your joy may be complete.
	aa′	**X**	5This is the message we *have heard from him* and *proclaim to you,* that God is light and in him is no darkness at all.
		Y	6*If we say we have fellowship with him while we walk in darkness*, we lie and do not live according to the truth;
		Y′	7abut *if we walk in the light* as he is in the light, we have *fellowship with him*
		X′	7band the blood of Jesus his *Son* cleanses us from all sin

JESUS THE ADVOCATE

			1 JOHN: SEGMENT B-A (1:8–2:2)		
a	aa	X	[1:8a]*If we say we have no sin,*		
		Y	[1:8b]we deceive ourselves,		
		X′	[1:8c]and the truth is *not in us*		
	bb	[9]If we confess our sins, he is faithful and just, and will forgive our sins and cleanse us from all unrighteousness			
	aa′	X	[10a]*If we say we have not sinned,*		
		Y	[10b]we make him a liar,		
		X′	[10c]and his word is *not in us*		
b	[2:1]My little children, I am writing this to you so that you may not sin, but if anyone does sin we have an advocate with the Father, Jesus Christ the righteous				
a′	[2:2]and he is the expiation for our sins, and not for ours only but also for the sins of the whole world.				

KEEP HIS COMMANDMENTS

		1 JOHN: SEGMENT B-B (2:3-11)		
a	**aa**	2:3 And *by this we may be sure* that *we know him*, if we *keep his* commandments		
	bb	4*He who says* "I know him" but disobeys his commandments is a liar, and the truth is not in him;		
	aa′	5Whoever *keeps his word; in him* truly love for God is perfected. *By this we may be sure* that *we are in him.*		
	bb′	6*He who says* he abides in him ought to walk in the same way in which he walked.		
b	**aa**	7Beloved, I am writing you no new commandment, but an *old commandment* which you had from the beginning;		
	bb	**The *old commandment* is the word which you have heard.**		
	aa′	**X**	8a Yet I am writing you a new commandment, which is *true in him* and in you,	
		Y	**8b because the darkness is passing away.**	
		X′	8c and the *true light* is already shining,	
a′	**aa**	2:9 *He who says* he is in the light and *hates his brother is in the darkness still.*		
	bb	**2:10 He who loves his brother abides in the light, and in it there is no cause for stumbling.**		
	aa′	2:11 But he who *hates his brother is in the darkness* and walks in the darkness, and does not know where he is going, because the darkness has blinded his eyes.		

THE BELIEVING COMMUNITY

1 JOHN: SUB-SEGMENT B-A′ (2:12–28)				
a			²:¹²I am writing to you, *little children*, because your sins are forgiven for his sake.	
	aa		²:¹³ᵃI am writing to you, fathers, because you know him who is from the beginning.	
	bb		¹³ᵇI am writing to you, young men, because you have overcome the evil one.	
	cc		¹³ᶜI write to you, children, because you know the Father.	
b	**aa′**		²:¹⁴ᵃI write to you, fathers, because you know him who is from the beginning.	
	bb′	**X**	¹⁴ᵇI write to you, young men, because you are strong	
		Y	¹⁴ᶜand the word of God abides in you,	
		X′	¹⁴ᵈand you have overcome the evil one.	
c	**aa**	**X**	²:¹⁵ᵃDo not love *the world* or the things in the world.	
		Y	¹⁵ᵇIf anyone loves the world, love for the Father is not in him	
		X′	**x**	¹⁶ᵃFor all that is *in the world*,
			y	¹⁶ᵇlust of the flesh and lust of the eyes and the pride of life
			x′	¹⁶ᶜ*Is not of the Father*, but *is of the world*
	aa′		¹⁷ᵃand the world *passes away*, and the lust in it;	
	bb		¹⁷ᵇbut he who does the will of God *abides forever*.	
d	**aa**	**X**	¹⁸ᵃChildren, *it is the last hour and* ¹⁸ᵇ*as you have heard that antichrist is coming*,	
		X′	*so now many antichrists have come.* ¹⁸ᶜtherefore, we know *that it is the last hour*	
		Y′	**x**	¹⁹ᵃ*They went out* from us, but they were *not of us*;
			y	¹⁹ᵇfor if they had been of us, they would have continued with us
			x′	¹⁹ᶜbut *they went out*, that it might be plain that they all *are not of us*
	bb	**X**	²:²⁰But you have been anointed by the Holy One, and you all know	
		Y	²:²¹ᵃI write to you, not because you do not know the truth, but because you know it,	

		X′	2:21b and you know that no lie comes from the truth
		X	2:22a Who is the *liar*, but *he who denies* that Jesus is the Christ.
	aa′	**Y**	2:22b This is the *antichrist, he who denies* the Father and the Son.
		X′	2:23 *No one who denies the Son has the Father. He who confesses the Son has the Father* also
c′	**aa**		2:24a Let *what you heard from the beginning abide in you.*
	aa′		2:24b If *what you heard from the beginning abides in you*, then you will abide in the Son and in the Father. 25 And this is what he has promised us, *eternal life*
	bb		26 I write this to you about those who would deceive you
b′	**aa**		2:27a as for you the anointing, which you received from him, *abides in you,*
	bb	**X**	2:27b and you have no need that any one should *teach you;* as his anointing teaches you about everything, and
		Y	2:27c is true and is no lie,
		X′	2:27d just as it has *taught you,*
	aa′		2:27e *abide in him.*
a′			2:28 And now, *little children*, abide in him, so that when he appears we may have confidence and not shrink from him in shame at his coming.

THE CHOICE: PURIFY OR SIN

		**1 JOHN: SEGMENT C (2:29–3:10)**		

a				[2:29]If you know that *he is righteous*, you may be sure that everyone *who does right* is *born of him*.
b	aa			[3:1a]See what love the Father has given us that we should be called *children of God*; and so *we are*.
	bb			[3:1b]The reason why the world does not know us is that it did *not know him*.
	aa′	X		[2]Beloved, we are *God's children* now it does "not yet" *appear* what *we shall,,*;
		X′		but we know that when he *appears we shall* be like him,
		Y		for we shall see him as *he is*.
c				[3]And everyone who thus hopes in him purifies himself as he is pure, [4]Everyone who commits sin is guilty of lawlessness; sin is lawlessness.
b′	aa	X		[5]You know that he *appeared* to take away sins, and in him there is no sin.
		Y		[6]*No one* who abides in him *sins*.
		Y′		No one who *sins* has either seen him or *known him*.
	bb			[7]Little children, let no one deceive you. He who does right is righteous, as he is righteous
	aa′	X	x	[8]He *who commits sin is of the devil*;
			x′	*for the devil has sinned* from the beginning.
			y	The reason the Son of God *appeared* was to destroy the works of the devil
		X′	x	[9a]No one born of God *commits sin*;
			y	[9b]for God's nature abides in him,
			x′	[9c]and he *cannot sin* because he is *born of God*.
		Y		[10a]By this it may be seen who are the children of God, and who are the children of the devil:
a′				[10b]whoever *does not do right* is not of God, nor he who does not love his brother

BELIEVE AND LOVE

			1 JOHN: SUB-SEGMENT B'-A (3:11-4:6)
a	aa	X	3:11For this is the message, which you have *heard from the beginning*, that we should love one another
		Y	12and not be like Cain who was of the *evil* one and *murdered his brother*.
		Y'	And why did he *murder him*? Because his own deeds were *evil* and his *brother's* righteous.
	bb	X	13Do not wonder, brethren, that the world hates you.
		Y	14aWe know that we have passed out of death into life, because we love the brethren.
		X'	14bHe who does not love abides in death.
	aa'	X	15Anyone who hates *his brother* is a murderer, and you know that no murderer has eternal life *abiding in him*.
		Y	16By this we know love that he laid down his life for us; and we ought to lay down our lives for the brethren.
		X'	17But if anyone has the world's goods and sees *his brother* in need, yet closes his heart against him, how does God's love *abide in him?* 18Little children, let us not love in word or speech but in deed and truth.
b	aa		3:19aBy this we shall know that we are of the truth
	bb	X	3:19bReassure our hearts before him, 20whenever *our hearts condemn us*; *for God* is greater than our hearts, and he knows everything
		X'	21Beloved, if *our hearts do not condemn us*, we have confidence *before God*.
		Y	22aand we receive from him whatever we ask.
	aa'	X	3:22bbecause *we keep his commandments* and do what pleases him.
		Y	3:23And this is his commandment that we should believe in the name of his Son Jesus Christ and love one another, just as he has commanded us
		X'	24aAll who *keep his commandments* abide in him, and he in them.

	aa		[24b]And *by this we know* that he abides in us, *by the Spirit*, which he has given us.
	bb		[4:1]Beloved don't believe every spirit, but test the spirits to see whether they are of God, for many false prophets have gone out into the world·
a'	**cc**	**X**	[4:2]By this you know the Spirit of God: *every spirit, which confesses that Jesus Christ has come in the flesh is of God,*
		X'	[4:3]and *every spirit which does not confess Jesus is not of God.* This is the spirit of antichrist, of which you heard that it was coming, and now it is in the world already.
		Y	[4:4]Little children, you are of God, and have overcome them; for he who is in you is greater than he who is in the world.
	bb'	**X**	[4:5]They are *of the world*, therefore what they say is *of the world*, and the world listens to them.
		Y	[4:6a]*We are of God. Whoever knows God listens to us,*
		Y'	and *he who* is *not of God does not listen to us*
	aa'		[4:6b]By this we know the spirit of truth and the spirit of error

Why Love and Believe in Jesus

			1 John: Segment B′–b (4:7–5:3)			
a	**aa**	**X**		*4:7*Beloved, let us *love one another*;		
		Y		for *love is of God and he who loves* is born of God and *knows God*.		
		Y′		*8He who does not love does not know God*; for *God is love*.		
	bb	**X**		*9aIn this the love* of God was made manifest among us that God *sent his only Son* into the world,		
		Y		*9b*so that we might live through him.		
		X′		*10In this is love*, not that we loved God but that he loved us and *sent his Son* to be the expiation for our sins.		
	aa′	**X**		*11*Beloved, if God so loved us, we also ought to *love one another*		
		Y		*12a*No man has ever seen God;		
		X′	**x**	*12bif we love one another*, God abides in us and his *love is perfected in us*.		
			y	*13a* By this *we know* that we *abide in him* and *he in us*,		
			x′	*13b*because he has given us of his own Spirit.		
b				*14And we have seen and testify that the Father has sent his Son as the Savior of the world.*		
a′	**aa**	**X**	**x**	*15Whoever confesses that Jesus is the Son of God, God abides in him*, and *he in* God.		
			y	*16a*So we know and believe the *love God has for us*.		
			x′	*16bGod is love*, and he who abides in love *abides in God, God abides in us*.		
		Y	**x**	*17aIn this is love perfected with us*		
			y	*17bthat we may have confidence for the day of judgment, because as he is so are we in this world.*		
			x′		**xx**	*18aThere is no fear in love*,
					yy	*18bbut perfect love* casts out fear.

		xx′	[18c]For fear has to do with punishment, and he who *fears is not perfected in love.*
	X′		[19]We love, because *he first loved us*
bb	**X**		[20]If any one says, "I *love God*," and *hates his brother*, he is a liar;
	X′		For he who does not *love his brother* whom he has seen *cannot love God* whom he has not seen.
	Y		[21]And this commandment we have from him, that he who loves God should love his brother also.
aa′	**X**		[5:1]Everyone who believes that Jesus is the Christ is a child of God, and everyone who loves the parent loves the child.
	Y		[2]By this we know that we love the children of God, when *we love God and obey his commandments.*
	Y′		[3]For this is the *love of God, that we obey his commandments.* And his commandments are not burdensome.

FAITH

1 JOHN: SEGMENT B′–C (5:4–5)	
a	[5:4a]For whatever is born of God *overcomes the world;*
b	**[4b]and this is the victory that overcomes the world, our faith.**
a′	[5]Who is it that *overcomes the world* but he who believes that Jesus is the Son of God.

JESUS CHRIST THE SON OF GOD IS FULLY HUMAN

	1 JOHN: SEGMENT B'–B' (5:6-13)		
a	**aa**	**X**	5:6aThis is he who came *by water and blood,*
		Y	6bJesus Christ
		X'	6cnot with the water only but with the *water and the blood.*
	bb		7And the Spirit is *the witness,* because the Spirit is the truth.
	aa'	**X**	5:8aThere are *three witnesses,*
		Y	8bthe Spirit, *the water, and the blood*;
		X'	8cand *these three* agree.
b	**aa**		9If we receive the *testimony* of men, the *testimony of God* is greater; for this is *the testimony of God that he has borne witness to his Son.*
	bb		10a*He who believes in the Son of God* has the testimony in himself.
	aa'		10b*He who does not believe God* has made him a liar, because he has not believed in *the testimony that God has borne to his Son*
b'	**aa**		11And *this is the testimony: that God* gave us *eternal life* and *this life is in the Son*
	aa'		12*he who has the Son has life; he who has not the Son of God has not life.*
	bb		5:13I write this to you *who believe in the name of the Son of God,* that you may know that you have eternal life.

ASK AND RECEIVE

I JOHN: SEGMENT B'–A' (5:14–17)		
a		5:14And this is the confidence, which we have in him, that *if we ask* anything according to his will *he hears us.*
a'		5:15And if we know that *he hears us* in whatever *we ask*, we know that we have obtained the request*s* made of him.
b	aa	5:16aIf any one sees his brother committing *what is not a mortal sin*
	bb	16bhe will ask, and God will give him life for those whose sin is not mortal.
	aa'	16cThere is sin which is mortal. I do not say that one is to pray for that. 17All wrongdoing is sin, but there is sin, *which is not mortal.*

ETERNAL LIFE DEFINED

I JOHN: SEGMENT A' (5:18–21)		
a	aa	5:18a*We know* that any one born *of God* does not sin,
	bb	18bbut He who was born of God keeps him, and the evil one does not touch him
	aa'	19*We know* that we are *of God*, and the whole world is in the power of the evil one.
a'	aa	5:20And we know that *the Son of God* has come and has given us understanding, *to know him who is true;*
	aa'	and we are *in him who is true, in his Son Jesus Christ.*
	bb	This is the true God and eternal life.
b		5:21Little children, keep yourselves from idols

REJECT ALL FALSE TEACHING

	**2 JOHN 1–13**

A	**a**	[1:1]The elder to the *elect lady* and *her children*, whom I love in *the truth*, and not only I but also all who know *the truth*, [2]because of the truth which abides in us and will be with us forever:
	b	**[3a]Grace, mercy, and peace will be with us, from God the Father and from Jesus Christ the Father's Son,**
	a′	[3b]in truth and love.
B		[4]I rejoiced greatly to find some of *your children* ~~following~~ walking in the truth, just as we have been commanded by the Father
C	**a**	[5]And now I beg you, lady, not as though I were writing you a new *commandment*, but the one *we have had from the beginning,* that *we love one another*
	b	**[6a]And this is love, that we walk according to his commandments**
	a′	[6b]this is the *commandment, as you have heard from the beginning,* that you *follow love.*

B′	**a**	**X**	[7a]For *many deceivers* have gone into the world
		Y	**[7b]men who will not acknowledge the coming of Jesus Christ in the flesh;**
		X′	[7c]such a *one is the deceiver* and the antichrist.
	b		**[8]Look to yourselves that you may not lose what you have worked for, but may win a full reward.**
	a′	**X**	[9]Anyone who goes ahead and *does not abide in the doctrine* of Christ *does not have God*;
		X′	he who abides in the doctrine has both the Father and the Son.
		Y	**[10]If any one comes to you and does not bring this doctrine, do not receive him into the house or give him any greeting; [11]for he who greets him shares his wicked work.**

A′	[12]Though I have much to write to you, I would rather not use paper and ink, but I hope to come to see you and talk with you face to face, so that *our joy* may be complete. [13]*The children* of your *elect sister* greet you.

LOVE ALL OF YOUR BRETHREN

3 JOHN 1–15					
A	a		*1*The elder to the beloved Ga'ius, whom I love in the truth.		
	b		*2a*Beloved, I pray that all may go well with you and that you may be in health;		
	a′		*2b*I know that it is well with your soul.		
B	a	X	*3*For I greatly rejoiced when some of the brethren arrived and *testified to the truth* of your life, as indeed you do ~~follow~~ walk in the truth.		
		Y	*4*No greater joy can I have than this, to hear that my *children* ~~follow~~ *walk in the truth.*		
		X′	*5*Beloved, it is a loyal thing you do when you render any service to the brethren, especially to strangers, *6a*who have *testified to your love* before the church.		
	b		*6b*You will do well to send them on their journey as befits God's service. *7*For they have set out for his sake and have accepted nothing from the heathen.		
	a′		*8*So we ought to support such men, that we may be fellow workers *in the truth.*		
C	a	X	*9*I have written something to the church; but Diot'rephes, who likes to put himself first, does not accept my authority		
		Y	*10a*So if I come, I will bring up what he is doing, prating against me with evil words		
		X′	x	*10b*And not content with that, he refuses himself to welcome the brethren,
			y	*10c*and also stops those that want to welcome them
			x′	*10d*and puts them out of the church.
	b		*11a*Beloved, do not imitate *evil*		
	c		*11b*but imitate good.		
	c′		He who does good is of God;		
	b′		*11c*he who does evil has not seen God.		
B′			*12*Deme'trius has *testimony* from everyone, and *from the truth* itself; I testify to him too, and you know *my testimony is true*		
A′			*13*I had much to write to you, but I would rather not write with pen and ink; *14*I hope to see you soon, and we will talk together face to face. *15*Peace be to you. The friends greet you. Greet the friends, every one of them by name.		

1, 2, 3 John

RSV

1 John

CHAPTER 1

WHAT WAS FROM THE BEGINNING

1:1aThat which was from the beginning, 1:1bwhich we have heard, 1:1cwhich we have seen with our eyes, which we have looked upon and touched with our hands, concerning the word of life. 2athe life was made manifest, 2band we saw it, and testify to it, and proclaim to you the eternal life, 2cwhich was with the Father and was made manifest to us 3athat which we have seen and heard we proclaim also to you, 3bso that you may have fellowship with us 3cand our fellowship is with the Father and with his Son Jesus Christ. 4And we are writing this that our joy may be complete.

WALKING IN DARKNESS OR IN THE LIGHT

1:5aThis is the message we have heard from him and proclaim to you, that God is light and in him is no darkness at all. 6If we say we have fellowship with him while we walk in darkness, we lie and do not live according to the truth; 7abut if we walk in the light, as he is in the light, we have fellowship with one another, 7band the blood of Jesus his Son cleanses us from all sin. 8If we say we have no sin, we deceive ourselves, and the truth is not in us. 9: If we confess our sins, he is faithful and just, and will forgive our sins and cleanse us from all unrighteousness. 10If we say we have not sinned, we make him a liar, and his word is not in us.

CHAPTER 2

WALKING JUST AS HE WALKED

2:1My little children, I am writing this to you so that you may not sin; but if any one does sin, we have an advocate with the Father, Jesus Christ the righteous; 2and he is the expiation for our sins, and not for ours only but also for the sins of the whole world. 3And by this we may be sure that we know him, if we keep his commandments. 4He who says "I know him" but disobeys his commandments, is a liar, and the truth is not in him; 5 but whoever keeps his word, in him truly love for

God is perfected. By this we may be sure that we are in him: [6]he who says he abides in him ought to walk in the same way in which he walked.

A COMMANDMENT OLD, YET NEW

[7]Beloved, I am writing you no new commandment, but an old commandment which you had from the beginning; the old commandment is the word which you have heard. [8]Yet I am writing you a new commandment, which is true in him and in you, because the darkness is passing away and the true light is already shining. [9]He who says he is in the light and hates his brother is in the darkness still. [10]He who loves his brother abides in the light, and in it there is no cause for stumbling. [11]But he who hates his brother is in the darkness and walks in the darkness, and does not know where he is going, because the darkness has blinded his eyes.

THE FAMILY RESTORED

[12]I am writing to you, little children, because your sins are forgiven for his sake. [13]I am writing to you, fathers, because you know him who is from the beginning. I am writing to you, young men, because you have overcome the evil one. I write to you, children, because you know the Father. [14]I write to you, fathers, because you know him who is from the beginning. I write to you, young men, because you are strong, and the word of God abides in you, and you have overcome the evil one.

THE WORLD VERSUS THE WILL OF GOD

[15]Do not love the world or the things in the world. If anyone loves the world, love for the Father is not in him. [16]For all that is in the world, the lust of the flesh and the lust of the eyes and the pride of life, is not of the Father but is of the world. [17]And the world passes away, and the lust of it; but he who does the will of God abides forever.

ENDURANCE AMID ANTICHRIST'S COMING

[18]Children, it is the last hour; and as you have heard that antichrist is coming, so now many antichrists have come; therefore we know that it is the last hour. [19]They went out from us, but they were not of us; for if they had been of us, they would have continued with us; but they went out, that it might be plain that they all are not of us. [20]But you have been anointed by the Holy One, and you all know. [21]I write to you, not because you do not know the truth, but because you know it, and know that no lie comes from the truth. [22]Who is the liar but he who denies that Jesus is the Christ? This is the antichrist, he who denies the Father and the Son. [23]No one who denies the Son has the Father. He who confesses the Son has the Father also. [24]Let what you heard from the beginning abide in you. If what you

heard from the beginning abides in you, then you will abide in the Son and in the Father. [25]And this is what he has promised us, eternal life.

ANOINTING THE TRUTH

[26]I write this to you about those who would deceive you. [27]As for you, the anointing which you received from him abides in you, and you have no need that any one should teach you; as his anointing teaches you about everything, and is true, and is no lie, just as it has taught you, abide in him.

CONFIDENCE AT CHRIST'S COMING

[28]And now, little children, abide in him, so that when he appears we may have confidence and not shrink from him in shame at his coming. [29]If you know that he is righteous, you may be sure that everyone who does right is born of him.

CHAPTER 3

CHILDREN OF GOD

[3:1]See what love the Father has given us that we should be called children of God; and so we are. The reason why the world does not know us is that it did not know him. [2]Beloved, we are God's children now; it does "not yet" appear what we shall be [possibility for sin now and in the state of not yet], but we know that when he appears we shall be like him, for we shall see him as he is. [3]And everyone who thus hopes in him purifies himself as he is pure.

CHILDREN OF GOD OR CHILDREN OF THE DEVIL

[4]Everyone who commits sin is guilty of lawlessness; sin is lawlessness. [5]You know that he appeared to take away sins, and in him there is no sin. [6]No one who abides in him sins; no one who sins has either seen him or known him. [7]Little children, let no one deceive you. He who does right is righteous as he is righteous. [8]He who commits sin is of the devil; for the devil has sinned from the beginning. The reason the Son of God appeared was to destroy the works of the devil. [9]No one born of God commits sin; for God's nature abides in him, and he cannot sin because he is born of God. [10]By this it may be seen who the children of God are and who are the children of the devil: whoever does not do right is not of God, nor he who does not love his brother.

THE MESSAGE YOU HAVE HEARD FROM THE BEGINNING
BY THIS WE KNOW LOVE

[11]For this is the message, which you have heard from the beginning, that we should love one another, [12]and not be like Cain who was of the evil one and murdered his brother. And why did he murder him? Because his own deeds were evil and his brother's righteous. [13]Do not wonder, brethren, that the world hates you. [14]We know that we have passed out of death into life, because we love the brethren. He who does not love abides in death. [15]Anyone who hates his brother is a murderer, and you know that no murderer has eternal life abiding in him. [16]By this we know love that he laid down his life for us; and we ought to lay down our lives for the brethren. [17]But if anyone has the world's goods and sees his brother in need, yet closes his heart against him, how does God's love abide in him? [18]Little children, let us not love in word or speech but, in deed and in truth.

BY THIS WE SHALL KNOW THAT WE ARE OF THE TRUTH

[19]By this we shall know that we are of the truth, and reassure our hearts before him [20]whenever our hearts condemn us; for God is greater than our hearts, and he knows everything. [21]Beloved, if our hearts do not condemn us, we have confidence before God; [22]and we receive from him whatever we ask, because we keep his commandments and do what pleases him. [23]And this is his commandment that we should believe in the name of his Son Jesus Christ and love one another, just as he has commanded us. [24]All who keep his commandments abide in him, and he in them. And by this we know that he abides in us, by the Spirit, which he has given us.

CHAPTER 4

BY THIS YOU KNOW THE SPIRIT OF GOD

[4:1]Beloved don't believe every spirit, but test the spirits to see whether they are of God; for many false prophets have gone out into the world. [2]By this you know the Spirit of God: every spirit, which confesses that Jesus Christ has come in the flesh is of God, [3]and every spirit which does not confess Jesus is not of God. This is the spirit of antichrist, of which you heard that it was coming, and now it is in the world already. [4]Little children, you are of God, and have overcome them; for he who is in you is greater than he who is in the world. [5]They are of the world, therefore what they say is of the world, and the world listens to them. [6]We are of God. Whoever knows God listens to us, and he who is not of God does not listen to us. By this we know the spirit of truth and the spirit of error.

BY THIS GOD'S LOVE WAS MANIFESTED AMONG US

[7]Beloved, let us love one another; for love is of God, and he who loves is born of God and knows God. [8]He who does not love does not know God; for God is love. [9]In this the love of God was made manifest among us that God sent his only Son into the world, so that we might live through him. [10]In this is love, not that we loved God but that he loved us and sent his Son to be the expiation for our sins. [11]Beloved, if God so loved us, we also ought to love one another. [12]No man has ever seen God; if we love one another, God abides in us and his love is perfected in us.

BY THIS WE KNOW THAT WE ABIDE IN GOD AND GOD IN US

[13]By this we know that we abide in him and he in us, because he has given us of his own Spirit. [14]And we have seen and testify that the Father has sent his Son as the Savior of the world. [15]Whoever confesses that Jesus is the Son of God, God abides in him, and he in God. [16]So we know and believe the love God has for us. God is love, and he who abides in love abides in God, and God abides in him. [17]In this is love perfected with us, that we may have confidence for the day of judgment, because as he is so are we in this world. [18]There is no fear in love, but perfect love casts out fear. For fear has to do with punishment, and he who fears is not perfected in love. [19]We love, because he first loved us. [20]If any one says, "I love God," and hates his brother, he is a liar; for he who does not love his brother whom he has seen, cannot love God whom he has not seen. [21]And this commandment we have from him, that he who loves God should love his brother also.

CHAPTER 5

BY THIS WE KNOW WE LOVE GOD'S CHILDREN

[1]Everyone who believes that Jesus is the Christ is a child of God, and everyone who loves the parent loves the child. [2]By this we know that we love the children of God, when we love God and obey his commandments. [3]For this is the love of God, that we keep his commandments. And his commandments are not burdensome. [4]For whatever is born of God overcomes the world; and this is the victory that overcomes the world, our faith. [5]Who is it that overcomes the world but he who believes that Jesus is the Son of God?

THE TESTIMONY THAT GOD HAS BORNE TO THE SON

[6]This is he who came by water and blood, Jesus Christ, not with the water only but with the water and the blood. [7]And the Spirit is the witness, because the Spirit is the truth. [8]There are three witnesses, the Spirit, the water, and the blood; and these three agree. [9]If we receive the testimony of men, the testimony of God is

greater; for this is the testimony of God that he has borne witness to his Son. [10]He who believes in the Son of God has the testimony in himself. He who does not believe God has made him a liar, because he has not believed in the testimony that God has borne to his Son. [11]And this is the testimony that God gave us eternal life, and this life is in his Son. [12]He who has the Son has life; he who has not the Son of God has not life.

THE BOLDNESS IN OUR ASKING

[13]I write this to you who believe in the name of the Son of God, that you may know that you have eternal life. [14]And this is the confidence, which we have in him, that if we ask anything according to his will he hears us. [15]And if we know that he hears us in whatever we ask, we know that we have obtained the requests made of him. [16]If any one sees his brother committing what is not a mortal sin, he will ask, and God will give him life for those whose sin is not mortal. There is sin which is mortal; I do not say that one is to pray for that. [17]All wrongdoing is sin, but there is sin, which is not mortal.

WHAT WE KNOW

[18]We know that any one born of God does not sin, but He who was born of God keeps him, and the evil one does not touch him. [19]We know that we are of God, and the whole world is in the power of the evil one. [20]And we know that the Son of God has come and has given us understanding, to know him who is true; and we are in him who is true, in his Son Jesus Christ. This is the true God and eternal life. [21]Little children, keep yourselves from idols.

2 John

^{1:1}The elder to the elect lady and her children, whom I love in the truth, and not only I but also all who know the truth, ²because of the truth which abides in us and will be with us for ever:

³Grace, mercy, and peace will be with us, from God the Father and from Jesus Christ the Father's Son, in truth and love.

BODY: REQUESTS, BENEFITS, AND CAUTIONS
LOVE ONE ANOTHER

⁴I rejoiced greatly to find some of your children following the truth, just as we have been commanded by the Father. ⁵And now I beg you, lady, not as though I were writing you a new commandment, but the one we have had from the beginning, that we love one another. ⁶And this is love, that we follow his commandments; this is the commandment, as you have heard from the beginning, that you follow love.

SPURN DECEPTION

⁷For many deceivers have gone out into the world, men who will not acknowledge the coming of Jesus Christ in the flesh; such a one is the deceiver and the antichrist. ⁸Look to yourselves that you may not lose what you have worked for, but may win a full reward.

BENEFITS AND CAUTIONS: ABIDE IN THE TEACHING

⁹Anyone who goes ahead and does not abide in the doctrine of Christ does not have God; he who abides in the doctrine has both the Father and the Son. ¹⁰If any one comes to you and does not bring this doctrine, do not receive him into the house or give him any greeting; ¹¹for he who greets him shares his wicked work.

CLOSING

¹²Though I have much to write to you, I would rather not use paper and ink, but I hope to come to see you and talk with you face to face, so that our joy may be complete. ¹³The children of your elect sister greet you.

3 John

OPENING: SALUTATION, PRAYER, REJOICING

[1]The elder to the beloved Ga'ius, whom I love in the truth. [2]Beloved, I pray that all may go well with you and that you may be in health; I know that it is well with your soul. [3]For I greatly rejoiced when some of the brethren arrived and testified to the truth of your life, as indeed you do follow the truth. [4]No greater joy can I have than this, to hear that my children follow the truth.

SUPPORTING GOD'S MISSIONARIES

[5]Beloved, it is a loyal thing you do when you render any service to the brethren, especially to strangers, [6]who have testified to your love before the church. You will do well to send them on their journey as befits God's service. [7]For they have set out for his sake and have accepted nothing from the heathen. [8]So we ought to support such men, that we may be fellow workers in the truth.

CONDEMNING DIOTREPHES

[9]I have written something to the church; but Diot'rephes, who likes to put himself first, does not acknowledge my authority. [10]So if I come, I will bring up what he is doing, prating against me with evil words. And not content with that, he refuses himself to welcome the brethren, and also stops those who want to welcome them and puts them out of the church.

COMMENDING DEMETRIUS

[11]Beloved, do not imitate evil but imitate good. He who does good is of God; he who does evil has not seen God. [12]Deme'trius has testimony from everyone, and from the truth itself; I testify to him too, and you know my testimony is true.

CLOSING: REGRETS, HOPES, AND GREETINGS

[13]I had much to write to you, but I would rather not write with pen and ink; [14]I hope to see you soon, and we will talk together face to face. [15]Peace be to you. The friends greet you. Greet the friends, every one of them.

Appendix D

1, 2, 3 John

Spiral Texts

1 John
(1:1–5:21)

PART 1

Gift of Eternal Life
(1:1–7; 5:18–21)

FELLOWSHIP WITH GOD

[1:1a]That, which was from the beginning, [1c]concerning the word of life, [1b]which we have heard, which we have seen with our eyes, which we have looked upon and touched with our hands. [1:3] That which we have seen and heard we proclaim also to you so that you may have fellowship with us, and our fellowship is with the Father and with his Son Jesus Christ.

WALK IN THE LIGHT

[1:5]This is the message we have heard from him and proclaim to you, that God is light and in him is no darkness at all [7b]and the blood of Jesus his Son cleanses us from all sin.

[1:6]If we say we have fellowship with him while we walk in darkness, we lie and do not live according to the truth; [7a]but if we walk in the light as he is in the light, we have fellowship with him. [4]And we are writing this that your joy may be complete.

THE GIFT OF ETERNAL LIFE

[1:2a]The life was made manifest, [2c] which was with the Father and was made manifest to us. [2b]We saw it and testify to it, and proclaim to you the eternal life.

THE BENEFITS OF ETERNAL LIFE

5:18aWe know that any one born of God does not sin. 19We know that we are of God, and the whole world is in the power of the evil one, 18bbut he who was born of God keeps him, and the evil one does not touch him. 20And we know that the Son of God has come and has

given us understanding, to know him who is true; and we are in him who is true, in his Son Jesus Christ. This is the true God and eternal life.

THE CHALLENGE

5:21Little children, keep yourselves from idols.

PART 2

Believe and Love

(1:8–2:29; 3:11-5:17)

JESUS THE ADVOCATE
(1:8–2:2)

CONFESS

1:8aIf we say we have no sin 8cand the truth is not in us, 8bwe deceive ourselves. 10aIf we say we have not sinned 10cand his word is not in us, 10bwe make him a liar. 1:9If we confess our sins, he is faithful and just, and will forgive our sins and cleanse us from all unrighteousness; 2:2and he is the expiation for our sins, and not for ours only but also for the sins of the whole world.

JESUS THE ADVOCATE

2:1My little children, I am writing this to you so that you may not sin; but if anyone does sin, we have an advocate with the Father, Jesus Christ the righteous.

THE BELIEVING COMMUNITY
(2:12–2:28)

TO THE ENTIRE BELIEVING COMMUNITY

$^{2:12}$I am writing to you, little children, because your sins are forgiven for his sake. $^{2:28}$And now, little children, abide in him, so that when he appears we may have confidence and not shrink from him in shame at his coming.

TO BELIEVERS BORN OF GOD

$^{2:13a}$I am writing to you, fathers, because you know him who is from the beginning. ^{14a}I write to you, fathers, because you know him who is from the beginning.

$^{2:13b}$I am writing to you, young men, because you have overcome the evil one. ^{14b}I write to you, young men, because you are strong, ^{14d}and you have overcome the evil one, ^{14c}and the word of God abides in you.

^{13c}I write to you, children, because you know the Father. $^{2:27a}$As for you, the anointing which you received from him abides in you; $^{2:27e}$ abide in him. $^{2:27b}$And you have no need that any one should teach you; as his anointing teaches you about everything, $^{2:27d}$and just as it has taught you, $^{2:27c}$is true and is no lie.

TO BELIEVERS NOT YET BORN OF GOD

$^{2:15a}$Do not love the world or the things in the world. ^{16a}For all that is in the world, ^{16c}is not of the Father but is of the world, ^{16b}lust of the flesh and lust of the eyes and the pride of life. ^{15b}If anyone loves the world, love for the Father is not in him. ^{17}The world passes away, and the lust in it; but he who does the will of God abides forever.

$^{2:24}$Let what you heard from the beginning abide in you. If what you heard from the beginning abides in you, then you will abide in the Son and in the Father. ^{25}And this is what he has promised us, eternal life.

^{26}I write this to you about those who would deceive you

BELIEVERS WHO NO LONGER BELIEVE—THE ANTICHRISTS

2:18Children, it is the last hour and as you have heard that antichrist is coming, so now many antichrists have come; therefore we know that it is the last hour.

2:19aThey went out from us, but they were not of us; 19cbut they went out, that it might be plain that they all are not of us; 19bfor if they had been of us, they would have continued with us.

2:22aWho is the liar but he who denies that Jesus is the Christ? 23No one who denies the Son has the Father. He who confesses the Son has the Father also. 22bThis is the antichrist, he who denies the Father and the Son.

TO BELIEVERS BORN OF GOD—LET THE ANTICHRISTS GO

2:20But you have been anointed by the Holy One, and you all know. 21bYou know that no lie comes from the truth. 21aI write to you, not because you do not know the truth, but because you know it.

KEEP HIS COMMANDMENTS
(2:3–11)

WALK IN THE LIGHT—KEEP HIS COMMANDMENTS
& LOVE YOUR BROTHER

2:3And by this we may be sure that we know him, if we keep his commandments. 5Whoever keeps his word, in him truly love for God is perfected. By this we may be sure that we are in him.

2:4He who says "I know him" but disobeys his commandments, is a liar, and the truth is not in him. 6He who says he abides in him ought to walk in the same way in which he walked. 9He who says he is in the light and hates his brother is in the darkness still. 11He who hates his brother is in the darkness and walks in the darkness, and does not know where he is going, because the darkness has blinded his eyes.

²:¹⁰He who loves his brother abides in the light, and in it there is no cause for stumbling.

THE TRUE LIGHT AND A NEW COMMANDMENT

²:⁷ᵃBeloved, I am writing you no new commandment, but an old commandment, which you had from the beginning. ⁸Yet I am writing you a new commandment, which is true in him and in you. The true light is already shining because the darkness is passing away. ⁷ᵇThe old commandment is the word, which you have heard.

THE NEW COMMANDMENT: BELIEVE AND LOVE

LOVE AND BELIEVE IN THE SON JESUS CHRIST
(3:11–4:6; 5:14–17)

LOVE ONE ANOTHER

³:¹¹For this is the message, which you have heard from the beginning that we should love one another, ¹²and not be like Cain who was of the evil one and murdered his brother. And why did he murder him? Because his own deeds were evil and his brother's righteous. ¹⁵Anyone who hates his brother is a murderer, and you know that no murderer has eternal life abiding in him.

³:¹⁷If anyone has the world's goods and sees his brother in need, yet closes his heart against him, how does God's love abide in him? ¹⁸Little children, let us not love in word or speech, but in deed and in truth. ¹⁶By this we know love that he laid down his life for us; and we ought to lay down our lives for the brethren.

LOVE AND ETERNAL LIFE

³:¹³Do not wonder, brethren, that the world hates you. ¹⁴ᶜHe who does not love abides in death. ¹⁴ᵃᵇWe know that we have passed out of death into life, because we love the brethren. ²⁴ᵇᶜAnd by this we know that he abides in us, by the Spirit, which he has given us.

THE SPIRIT OF TRUTH AND THE SPIRIT OF ERROR

[4:6d]By this we know the spirit of truth and the spirit of error: [4:1]Beloved don't believe every spirit, but test the spirits to see whether they are of God; for many false prophets have gone out into the world. [5]They are of the world, therefore what they say is of the world, and the world listens to them. [6]We are of God. Whoever knows God listens to us, and he who is not of God does not listen to us.

[4:2]By this you know the Spirit of God: every spirit, which confesses that Jesus Christ has come in the flesh is of God, [3]and every spirit which does not confess Jesus is not of God. This is the spirit of antichrist, of which you heard that it was coming, and now it is in the world already.

[4:4]Little children, you are of God, and have overcome them; for he who is in you is greater than he who is in the world.

THE FATHER'S COMMANDMENT

[3:19]By this we shall know that we are of the truth, [22b]because we keep his commandments and do what pleases him. [24]All who keep his commandments abide in him, and he in them. [23]And this is his commandment: that we should believe in the name of his Son Jesus Christ and love one another, just as he has commanded us.

ASK AND RECEIVE

[3:19b]Reassure our hearts before him [20]whenever our hearts condemn us; for God is greater than our hearts, and he knows everything, [22a]and we receive from him whatever we ask. [21]Beloved, if our hearts do not condemn us, we have confidence before God, [22a]and we receive from him whatever we ask.[5:14]And this is the confidence, which we have in him, that if we ask anything according to his will he hears us. [15]And if we know that he hears us in whatever we ask, we know that we have obtained the requests made of him.

[3:16a]If any one sees his brother committing what is not a mortal sin ([16d]there is sin which is mortal) I do not say that one is to pray for that. [17]All wrongdoing is sin, but there is sin, which is not mortal. [16b]He will ask, and God will give him life for those whose sin is not mortal.

GOD'S PLAN

THE GOAL: LOVE ONE ANOTHER TO BE BORN OF GOD

[4:7]Beloved let us love one another; for love is of God, and he who loves is born of God and knows God. [8]He who does not love does not know God; for God is love.

[4:11]Beloved, if God so loved us, we also ought to love one another,[12b]if we love one another God abides in us and his love is perfected in us [13b]because he has given us of his own Spirit. [13a]By this we know that we abide in him and he in us.

THE APPROACH: GOD SENT HIS SON JESUS

[4:12a]No man has ever seen God. [9a]In this, the love of God was made manifest among us that God sent his only Son into the world. [10]In this is love, not that we loved God but that he loved us and sent his Son to be the expiation for our sins, [9b]so that we might live through him.

WHO IS JESUS?

JESUS IS THE SON OF GOD

[4:15]Whoever confesses that Jesus is the Son of God, God abides in him, and he in God. [16b]God is love, and he who abides in love abides in God. God abides in us [16a]so we know and believe the love God has for us. [19]We love, because he first loved us.

[4:17a]In this is love perfected with us; [18a]there is no fear in love [18c]for fear has to do with punishment, and he who fears is not perfected in love; [18b]but perfect love casts out fear [17bc]that we may have confidence for the day of judgment, because as he is so are we in this world.

JESUS THE SON OF GOD IS THE CHRIST

5:1Everyone who believes that Jesus is the Christ is a child of God, and everyone who loves the parent loves the child. 2By this we know that we love the children of God, when we love God and obey his commandments. 3For this is the love of God, that we obey his commandments. And his commandments are not burdensome.

4:20If anyone says, "I love God," and hates his brother, he is a liar; for he who does not love his brother whom he has seen cannot love God whom he has not seen. 21And this commandment we have from him, that he who loves God should love his brother also.

JESUS CHRIST THE SON OF GOD IS THE FULLY HUMAN SAVIOR

4:14And we have seen and testify that the Father has sent his Son as the Savior of the world. 5:6This is he who came by water and blood, not with the water only but with the water and the blood, Jesus Christ. 8There are three witnesses, and these three agree, the Spirit, the water, and the blood.

TESTIMONY AND FAITH

WITNESS AND TESTIMONY

5:7And the Spirit is the witness, because the Spirit is the truth. 5:9If we receive the testimony of men, the testimony of God is greater; for this is the testimony of God that he has borne witness to his Son. 10bHe who does not believe God has made him a liar, because he has not believed in the testimony that God has borne to his Son.

5:10aHe who believes in the Son of God has the testimony in himself.5:11And this is the testimony; God gave us eternal life and this life is in the Son. He who has the Son has life; he who has not the Son of God has not life.

OUR FAITH OVERCOMES THE WORLD

5:13I write this to you who believe in the name of the Son of God, that you may know that you have eternal life. 5:4aFor whatever is born of God overcomes the world; 5who is it that overcomes the world but he who believes that Jesus is the Son of God and ⁴ᵇthis is the victory that overcomes the world, our faith.

PART 3
The Choice—Purify or Sin
(2:29–3:10)

THE GOAL IS TO BE BORN OF GOD

²:²⁹If you know that he is righteous, you may be sure that everyone who does right is born of him. ³:¹⁰ᵇWhoever does not do right is not of God, nor he who does not love his brother.

TO BECOME CHILDREN OF GOD

³:¹ᵃSee what love the Father has given us that we should be called children of God; and so we are. ²Beloved, we are God's children now; it does "not yet" appear what we shall, but we know that when he appears we shall be like him, for we shall see him as he is.

SIN IS THE WORLDLY CHALLENGE

³:¹ᵇThe reason why the world does not know us is that it did not know him. ⁵You know that he appeared to take away sins, in him there is no sin. ⁶No one who abides in him sins; no one who sins has either seen him or known him. ⁸He who commits sin is of the devil; for the devil has sinned from the beginning. The reason the Son of God appeared was to destroy the works of the devil.

RECEIVE GOD'S SEED

³:⁹ᵃNo one born of God commits sin, ⁹ᶜand he cannot sin because he is born of God; ⁹ᵇfor God's nature abides in him.

THE CHOICE: PURIFY OR SIN

³:¹⁰ᵃBy this it may be seen who the children of God are and who are the children of the devil. ⁷Little children, let no one deceive you. He who does right is righteous, as he is righteous. ³And everyone who thus hopes in him purifies himself as he is pure. ⁴Everyone who commits sin is guilty of lawlessness; sin is lawlessness.

2 John
(1:1–1:13)

WALKING IN THE TRUTH

^{1:1}The elder to the elect lady and her children, whom I love in the truth, and not only I but also all who know the truth, ²because of the truth which abides in us and will be with us forever, ^{3d}in truth and love. ^{3abc}Grace, mercy, and peace will be with us, from God the Father and from Jesus Christ the Father's Son.

^{1:12}Though I have much to write to you, I would rather not use paper and ink, but I hope to come to see you and talk with you face to face, so that our joy may be complete. ¹³The children of your elect sister greet you.

BEWARE OF THE DECEIVER WHO IS THE ANTICHRIST

^{1:4}I rejoiced greatly to find some of your children walking in the truth, just as we have been commanded by the Father, ⁷for many deceivers have gone out into the world. Such a one is the deceiver and the antichrist, men who will not acknowledge the coming of Jesus Christ in the flesh.

^{1:9}Anyone who goes ahead and does not abide in the doctrine of Christ does not have God; he who abides in the doctrine has both the Father and the Son. ¹⁰If any one comes to you and does not bring this doctrine, do not receive him into the house or give him any greeting; ¹¹for he who greets him shares his wicked work.

COMPLETE YOUR JOURNEY

^{1:8}Look to yourselves that you may not lose what you have worked for, but may win a full reward.

WALK ACCORDING TO HIS COMMANDMENTS

^{1:5}And now I beg you, lady, not as though I were writing you a new commandment, but the one we have had from the beginning, that we love one another. ^{6b}This is the commandment, as you have heard from the beginning, that you follow love. ^{1:6a}And this is love, that we follow his commandments.

3 John
(1:1–1:15)

INTRODUCTION

^{1:1}The elder to the beloved Ga'ius; whom I love in the truth. ^{2b}I know that it is well with your soul. ^{2a}Beloved, I pray that all may go well with you and that you may be in health.

¹³I had much to write to you, but I would rather not write with pen and ink; ¹⁴I hope to see you soon, and we will talk together face to face. ¹⁵Peace be to you. The friends greet you. Greet the friends, every one of them by name

GAIUS RENDERS SERVICE TO THE BRETHREN

^{1:3}For I greatly rejoiced when some of the brethren arrived and testified to the truth of your life, as indeed you do follow the truth. ⁵Beloved, it is a loyal thing you do when you render any service to the brethren, ^{6a}especially to strangers, who have testified to your love before the church. ⁴No greater joy can I have than this, to hear that my children follow the truth.

^{1:8}So we ought to support such men, that we may be fellow workers in the truth. ^{6bc}You will do well to send them on their journey as befits God's service. ⁷For they have set out for his sake and have accepted nothing from the heathen.

^{1:12}Deme'trius has testimony from everyone, and from the truth itself; I testify to him too, and you know my testimony is true.

DIOT'REPHES DOESN'T WELCOME THE BRETHREN

^{1:9}I have written something to the church; but Diot'rephes, who likes to put himself first, does not accept my authority. ^{10b}And not content with that, he refuses himself to welcome the brethren, ^{10d}and puts them out of the church ^{10c}and also stops those that want to welcome them. ^{10a}So if I come, I will bring up what he is doing, prating against me with evil words.

IMITATE GOOD

^{1:11a}Beloved, do not imitate evil (^{11c}he who does evil has not seen God) ^{11b}but imitate good. He who does good is of God.

Verse Locator

TABLE OF VERSE PAGES

VERSES	CH.	SPIRAL TEXT & COMMENTARY	CHIASTIC STRUCTURE	RSV TEXT	SPIRAL TEXT
1 John 1:1	3	35–37, 171	184	202	212
1:2	3	35, 39–42, 171–172	184	202	212
1:3	3	35–37, 174	184	202	212
1:4–5	3	35, 37–39, 175	184	202	212
1:6–7	3	35, 37–39, 175–176	184	203	212
1:8-2:2	4	56–65	185	202	213
2:3–6	6	77–80	186	203	215
2:7–8	6	77, 81–82	186	203	216
2:9–11	6	77–80	186	203	215
2:12	5	67, 69	188	203	214
2:13–14	5	67, 70–71	188	203	214

VERSES	CH.	SPIRAL TEXT & COMMENTARY	CHIASTIC STRUCTURE	RSV TEXT	SPIRAL TEXT
2:15-17	5	67, 71–72	188	203	214
2:18–19	5	67, 73–74	188	203	215
2:20–21	5	67, 74–75	188	203	215
2:22–23	5	67, 73–74	189	203	215
2:24	5	67, 71–72	189	203	214
2:25	5	67, 71–72	189	204	214
2: 26	5	67, 71–72	189	204	214
2:27	5	67, 70–71	189	204	214
2:28	5	67, 69	189	204	214
2:29	10	128–130	190	204	220
3:1-2	9	128, 130–131	190	204	220
3:3–4	9	129, 133	190	204	220
3:5–6	9	129, 131	190	204	220
3:7	9	129, 133	190	204	220
3:8	9	129, 131	190	204	220
3:9	9	129, 132	190	204	220

VERSES	CH.	SPIRAL TEXT & COMMENTARY	CHIASTIC STRUCTURE	RSV TEXT	SPIRAL TEXT
3:10a	9	128, 129–130	190	204	220
3:10b	9	126–128, 131	190	204	220
3:11–12	7	84, 86–87	192	205	216
3:13–14	7	84, 88	192	205	216
3:15–18	7	84, 86–87	192	205	216
3:19a	7	85, 91–92	192	205	217
3: 19b–22a	7	85, 92–96	192	205	217
3:22b–23	7	85, 91–92	192	205	217
3:24	7	85, 88, 91–92	192	205	217
4:1–6	7	84–85, 89–90	193	205	217
4:7–8	8	99, 102–103	194	206	218
4:9–10	8	100, 104–106	194	206	218
4:11	8	99, 103–104	194	206	218
4:12a	8	100, 104–106	194	206	218
4: 12b–13	8	99, 103–104	194	206	218
4:14	8	101, 111–115	194	206	219

VERSES	CH.	SPIRAL TEXT & COMMENTARY	CHIASTIC STRUCTURE	RSV TEXT	SPIRAL TEXT
4:15–18	8	100, 107–109	194	198	218
4:19	8	100, 107–109	195	206	218
4:20–21	8	100, 109–111	195	206	219
5:1–3	8	100, 109–111	195	206	218
5:4–5	8	101, 119	195	206	219
5:6	8	101, 111–113	196	206	219
5:7	8	101, 115, 118	196	206	219
5:8	8	101, 113–115	196	206	219
5:9–12	8	101, 115–118	196	207	219
5:13	8	101, 119	196	207	219
5:14–17	7	85, 92–96	197	207	217
5:18–20	3	36, 43–46, 177	197	207	213
5:21	3	36, 46, 177	197	207	213
2 John	10	142–149	198	208	221
3 John	11	151–156	199	209	223

Tables & Figures

TABLE OF TABLES

TABLE	DESCRIPTION	CH.	PG.
2-1	The "Good News" Message Is The New Covenant	2	27
3.1	Comparison Of Eternal Life Availability Before And After Jesus	3	45
6.1	Contrasting Effects Of Being And Not Being Born Of God	6	80
8.1	Progression From Faith To Knowing	8	117
8.2	Overview of 1 John	8	122
11.1	The People In The Letter	11	151
A-1	Repetitive Word Analysis 1 John 1:1–7	A	165
A-2	1 John 1:1–7 Text in Linear Order With Chiastic Labels	A	167
A-3	Spiral Text Sequence of 1 John 1:1–7	A	168
A-4	Three Types Of Parallel Relationships	A	169
A-5	Structure Of 1 John 1:1 With Synthetic Parallel Elements	A	171
A-6	Structure Of 1 John 1:2 With Synonymous Parallel Elements	A	172
A-7	Structure With Point of Prominence First	A	174
A-8	4–Part No Point of Prominence Chiastic Structure (1 John 1:5–7)	A	175
B-1	Chiastic Structure of 1 John	B	182

TABLE OF FIGURES

FIGURE	DESCRIPTION	CH.	PG.
1–1	How The Text Of John's 1st Letter Might Have Appeared	1	16
1–2	Matthew 7:6	1	17
1–3	Matthew 7:6 In Structural Form	1	18
1–4	Matthew 7:6 In Spiral Form	1	19
A–1	Matthew 7:6 In Structural Form	A.1	163
A–2	Matthew 7:6 In Spiral Form	A.1	163
A–3	Three Parts Of John's Typical Chiastic Structure	A.1	166

Index

CPSIA information can be obtained at www.ICGtesting.com
Printed in the USA
BVOW04s1407201113

336823BV00012B/364/P